THE PATRIARCHS
OF CONSTANTINOPLE

THE PATRIARCHS
OF CONSTANTINOPLE

BY

CLAUDE DELAVAL COBHAM, C.M.G.

WITH INTRODUCTIONS BY THE

Rev. ADRIAN FORTESCUE, Ph.D., D.D.

AND THE

Rev. H. T. F. DUCKWORTH, M.A.
PROFESSOR OF DIVINITY, TRINITY COLLEGE, TORONTO CANADA

Cambridge:
at the University Press
1911

CAMBRIDGE
UNIVERSITY PRESS

University Printing House, Cambridge CB2 8BS, United Kingdom

Cambridge University Press is part of the University of Cambridge.

It furthers the University's mission by disseminating knowledge in the pursuit of education, learning and research at the highest international levels of excellence.

www.cambridge.org
Information on this title: www.cambridge.org/9781316613054

© Cambridge University Press 1911

First published 1911
First paperback edition 2016

A catalogue record for this publication is available from the British Library

ISBN 978-1-316-61305-4 Paperback

CONTENTS

PREFATORY NOTE

The real Preface to this pamphlet is supplied by my learned and kind friends the Revs. Adrian Fortescue and H. T. F. Duckworth, but a few words from me are necessary to explain its origin and purport.

I do not claim an acquaintance with the original sources of the history of the Patriarchate of Constantinople. I do not know if the subject has received at later hands the treatment it deserves. But I lighted on a work entitled Πατριαρχικοὶ Πίνακες, by Manuel I. Gedeon, printed at Constantinople (without date of publication, but written between 1885 and 1890), containing short lives of the bishops of Constantinople from the Apostle St Andrew to Joakim III.[1] It is a useful book, but an index was wanting, and this I now supply in two forms, chronological and alphabetical, as well as a list of the Patriarchs who are numbered with the Saints. Besides this I have done little but summarise Gedeon's text.

It may be noted that ninety-five Patriarchs reigned for less than a year. Also that of 328 vacancies between A.D. 36 and 1884

---

[1] It received the *imprimatur* of the Imperial Ministry of Public Instruction 25 Rabi'al-awwal, 1304—Dec. 23, 1887.

140 were by deposition,

  41 by resignation,

    3 Patriarchs were poisoned,

    2   murdered,

    1   beheaded,

    1   blinded,

    1   drowned,

    1   hanged,

    1   strangled.

In all 191 : so that 137 only closed their term of office by a natural death.

After the fall of Jerusalem the Jews had leaders, at least in Alexandria and Tiberias, whom they called Patriarchs, and this office was recognized from the reign of Nerva to that of Theodosios II. (A.D. 420). Among Christians the bishop of Antioch was the first to be called Patriarch, but he probably shared the title with other leading metropolitans. Later it was held that 'as there are five senses,' so there should be five Patriarchs, Rome, Constantinople, Alexandria, Antioch, Jerusalem. From 1589 to 1700 the Patriarch of Moscow was reckoned the fifth—Rome had fallen away in 1054—but only in 1723 the Great Church recognized the canonicity of the Russian Synod.

Patriarchs were elected by a synod of the bishops of the province, acting under the consent, the counsel or perhaps the orders, of the Emperor. Nor was the practice changed after the Turkish conquest of Constantinople, and in 1741 a *firman* of Mahmud I. sanctioned an orderly procedure, providing (*inter alia*) that the candidate should first have the approval of the bishops of Heracleia, Cyzicos, Nicomedeia, Nicaia and Chalcedon.

The laity took some part, not well defined, in the election. The expenses amounted in 1769 to 150,000 francs, in 1869 to less than 500.

The order of consecration of a bishop, following the Fourth Canon of Nicaia, and according to the form prepared by Metrophanes, bishop of Nyssa (Euchologion Mega, 176), is performed by the Ἀρχιερεὺς and δύο συλλειτουργοί, elsewhere in the rubric called οἱ τρεῖς ἀρχιερεῖς. The earliest Patriarchs were generally priests or monks, and rarely before the fall of Constantinople chosen from among the bishops of the province: the translation of bishops from one see to another being held at least irregular. Latterly it has been the rule that they should have for at least seven years filled a metropolitical see within the province. The Patriarch-elect should be consecrated or installed by the bishop of Heracleia, or, in his absence, by the bishop of Caisareia.

An interval of more than four years occurred between the retirement of Athanasios II. and the appointment of Gennadios II., and again between the patriarchates of Antonios III. and Nicolaos II. M. Gedeon cannot say who ought to administer the affairs of the œcumenical throne during a vacancy.

The Patriarch-elect was received by the Byzantine Emperors in great state, and, after the fall of Constantinople, by the earliest Ottoman Sultans. He is still presented to the sovereign, but with little pomp or ceremony.

Disputes arising in sees other than his own should be referred to him for decision: generally, he may pronounce judgment in all questions between the Orthodox—and woe betide him who appeals from such judgment to a secular court. He may give the rights of σταυροπήγια to churches not already consecrated, though they may be in another province. He only can receive clerics from another province without an ἀπολυτήριον (letters dimissory) from their own diocesan.

Upon taking up his duties the new Patriarch sends a letter, called ἐνθρονιστικὴ, to his brother Patriarchs, to which they reply in letters called εἰρηνικαί.

Homonymous Patriarchs are distinguished by the name of their birthplace, the see they had held, or by a nickname, never by numbers.

Probably no series of men, occupying through nearly eighteen centuries an exalted position, claim so little personal distinction as the Patriarchs of Constantinople. The early bishops are mere names :—

S. Andrew, Apostle and Martyr	Laurentios
Stachys	Alypios
Onesimos	Pertinax
Polycarpos I	Olympianos
Plutarchos	Marcos I
Sedekion	Philadelphos
Diogenes	Cyriacos I
Eleutherios	Castinos
Felix	Eugenios I
Polycarpos II	Titos
Athenodorus	Dometios
Euzoios	Ruphinos

Probos. The twenty-fifth in order of time.

Metrophanes I, A.D. 315–325, who saw the foundation of Constantinople, was too old to attend the first œcumenical council, and was represented in it by his successor,

Alexander, who was to have communicated with Arius on the very day of the heresiarch's appalling death.

Paulos, thrice expelled and twice restored, his place being first filled by

Eusebios, the Arian bishop of Nicomedeia, who consecrated
S. Sophia: secondly by another Arian

Macedonios. Paulos was at last exiled to Armenia, and there
strangled with his own pall by Arians.

Macedonios[2] deposed, anathematised by second œcumenical
council, 381.

Eudoxios, Arian, bishop of Antioch. Consecrated S. Sophia,
Feb. 15, 360.

Demophilos

Evagrios, banished by Valens.

Gregorios I, bishop of Nazianzum. Censured at second œcumenical
council and resigned.

Maximos I, deposed as a heretic by the same council.

Nectarios, a senator of Tarsus, chosen while yet unbaptized, and
installed by 150 bishops of the same council, at the bidding
apparently of the Emperor Theodosios.

Ioannes Chryostomos, born at Antioch, twice banished, died
Sept. 14, 407, at Komana in Pontus. S. Sophia burnt, 404.

Arsacios, brother of the Patriarch Nectarios.

Atticos, consecrated in 415 the restored church of S. Sophia.

Sisinios I

Nestorios, the heresiarch, condemned as a monophysite by the
third general council, of Ephesus, 431. Exiled to an oasis in
Egypt, where he died, 440.

Maximianos

Proclos, bishop of Cyzicos.

Flavianos, died of wounds received at the 'robber-synod' of
Ephesus.

Anatolios, installed by Dioscuros of Alexandria, fourth œcumenical
council, of Chalcedon, 431, condemned the heresy of Eutyches:
crowned the Emperor Leo I.

Gennadios I

Acacios. The first quarrel between the Church of the East and
Pope Felix III. The 'Henoticon' of the Emperor Zenon.
The finding of the body of S. Barnabas, and the independence
of the Church of Cyprus, 478.

Phravitas

Euphemios, deposed and banished.

Macedonios II, deposed and banished.

(50) Timotheos I, Kelon.

Ioannes II, Cappadoces.

Epiphanios. Pope John II visited Constantinople.

Anthimos I, bishop of Trapezus, promoted by the Empress Theodora, deposed by Pope Agapetus.

Menas. Consecrated by Pope Agapetus. Menas in turn consecrated Pope Agathon. Controversy with Vigilius.

Eutychios[1]. Fifth œcumenical council, of Constantinople, 553. Second consecration of S. Sophia.

Ioannes IV, Nesteutes. A synod at Constantinople, 587, declared the patriarch 'œcumenical.'

Cyriacos

Thomas I

Sergios, monotholete. Incursion of the Avars, 626.

Pyrrhos[1], monothelete, deposed.

Pyrrhos[2]

Petros, monothelete.

Thomas II

Ioannes V

Constantinos I

Theodoros I[1], deposed by Constantine Pogonatus.

Gregorios I. Sixth œcumenical council, of Constantinople, 680, counted Pope Honorius among the monothelete heretics.

Theodoros I[2]

Paulos III. Council of Constantinople, 'Penthektes' or 'in Trullo II,' 692.

Callinicos I, blinded, and banished to Rome by Justinian II.

Cyros, deposed by Philippicus.

Ioannes VI, monothelete.

Germanos I, bishop of Cyzicos, a eunuch, resigned.

Anastasios. The Patriarchate of Constantinople now conterminous with the Byzantine Empire.

Constantinos II, bishop of Sylaion, blinded, shaved and beheaded by Constantine Copronymus.

Nicetas I, a slave.

Paulos IV, a Cypriot, resigned.

Tarasios, a layman. Seventh œcumenical council, of Nicaia, 787.

Nicephoros I, a layman, deposed and banished by Leo the Armenian.

Theodotos, illiterate. εἰκονομάχος.

Antonios I, Kasymatas ; a tanner, then bishop of Sylaion. εἰκονομάχος.

Ioannes VII, Pancration. εἰκονομάχος, deposed by Theodora.

Methodios I, bishop of Cyzicos, promoted by Theodora. First mention of M. Athos.

Ignatios[1], son of the Emperor Michael Rhangabe and Procopia, eunuch ; deposed and banished by Baidas. Conversion of the Bulgarians.

Photios[1], a layman, deposed and banished by Basil the Macedonian. Conversion of the Russians.

Ignatios[2], canonised by Rome. Fourth council, of Constantinople, 869.

Photios[2], deposed and confined to a monastery by Leo the Wise. Synod of 879.

Stephanos I, son of Basil the Macedonian and Eudocia.

Antonios II, Kauleas.

Nicolaos I[1], mysticos ; deposed by Leo the Wise.

Euthymios I, deposed and banished by Alexander.

Nicolaos I[2], restored by Constantine Porphyrogennetos.

Stephanos II, bishop of Amaseia ; eunuch.

Tryphon

Theophylactos, a lad of sixteen, eunuch. Son of Romanus Lecapenus. Conversion of the Hungarians.

Polyeuctos, eunuch.

Basileios I, Scamandrenos. Deposed by John Tzimisces.

Antonios III, Studites

Nicolaos II, Chrysoberges

Sisinios II

Sergios II. The Patriarch of Alexandria declared κριτὴς τῆς οἰκουμένης.

Eustathios

(**100**) Alexios, appointed by Basil II.

Michael I, Cerularios, appointed by Constantine IX, deposed and banished by Isaac Comnenos. Excommunicated by Papal legates (the see of Rome was vacant), July 16, 1054.

Constantinos III, Leuchoudes : eunuch.

Ioannes VIII, Xiphilinos
Cosmas I, Hierosolymites
Eustratios, eunuch.
Nicolaos III, Grammaticos
Ioannes IX, Agapetos
Leon, Styppe
Michael II, Kurkuas
Cosmas II, deposed by a synod of bishops.
Nicolaos IV, Muzalon, archbishop of Cyprus.
Theodotos
Neophytos I
Constantinos IV, Chliarenos
Lucas
Michael III, bishop of Anchialos.
Chariton
Theodosios I
Basileios II, Camateros, deposed by Isaac Angelus.
Nicetas II, Muntanes
Leontios
Dositheos, Patriarch of Jerusalem. (In 1192 five ex-Patriarchs were alive.)
Georgios II, Xiphilinos
Ioannes IX, Camateros. Latin conquest of Constantinople, April 12, 1204.
Michael IV, Antoreianos
Theodoros II, Copas
Maximos II
Manuel, Sarantenos
Germanos II
Methodios II
Manuel II
Arsenios[1]
Nicephoros II
Arsenios[2]
Germanos III, present (after his deposition) at the second council of Lyons, 1274.
Ioseph I[1]
Ioannes XI, Beccos

Joseph I[2]

Gregorios II, a Cypriot.

Athanasios I[1]

Ioannes XII, Cosmas

Athanasios I[2]

Nephon I

Ioannes XIII, Glykys, a layman.

Gerasimos I

Hesaias

Ioannes XIV, Calekas

Isidoros

Callistos I[1]

Philotheos[1]

Callistos I[2]

Philotheos[2]

Macarios[1]

Neilos

Antonius IV[1], Macarios

Macarios[2]

(**150**) Antonios IV[2]

Callistos II

Matthaios I, sent the monk Joseph Bryennios to Cyprus, 1405.

Euthymios II

Joseph II, metropolitan of Ephesus: died at Florence, 1439, during the Council.

Metrophanes II, metropolitan of Cyzicos.

Gregorios III, died at Rome, 1459.

Athanasios II, resigned, 1450. Fall of Constantinople, May 29, 1453. [The vestments and ornaments of the Patriarch, imitated from those of the Byzantine Court, could hardly have been assumed before the fall of the city.]

Gennadios II, Scholarios, resigned May, 1456.

Isidoros II

Sophronios I, Syropulos

Ioasaph I, Kokkas: thrust forth about 1466 because he would not sanction the marriage of a Christian girl to a Moslem courtier. The Sultan, Mohammed II, spat in his face, and mowed away his beard with his sword. The Patriarch threw himself down a well.

Marcos II, Xylocaraves.

Dionysios I[1]. [The Lazes for a thousand florins buy the Patriarchate for Symeon, a monk of Trebizond. He gave way to Dionysios, metropolitan of Philippopolis, for whom Marus, mother of Sultan Bayazid, bought the Patriarchate for 2000 sequins: after a reign of five years he was rejected as a eunuch. Symeon was recalled, and the synod paid 2000 sequins; but the Serb Raphael offered 2500. Symeon was deposed, and Raphael, an unlettered sot, succeeded; but as the money was not paid he was led chained hand and foot through the city to beg it from his flock: he failed, and died in prison.]

Symeon[1]

Raphael

Maximos III

Symeon[2]

Nephon II[1]

Dionysios I[2]

Maximos IV, paid 2500 florins.   Deposed and died at M. Athos.

Nephon II[2]

Ioakeim I[1]

Nephon II[3]

Pachomios I[1]

Ioakeim I[2]

Pachomios I[2], poisoned by a servant.

Theoleptos I, bishop of Ioannina.

Ieremias I[1], bishop of Sophia: visited Cyprus, 1520.

Ioannikios I

Hieremias I[2]

Dionysios II[1]

Hieremias I[3]

Dionysios II[2]

Ioasaph II, metropolitan of Adrianople.

Metrophanes III[1], metropolitan of Caisareia.

Hieremias II[1], Tranos, metropolitan of Larissa.

Metrophanes III[2]

Hieremias II[2], banished to Rhodes.

Pachomios II, Palestos: banished to Wallachia.

Theoleptos II

Hieremias II[3]

Matthaios II[1]

Gabriel I

Theophanes I, Carykes, metropolitan of Athens.

[*Meletios Pegas, Patriarch of Alexandria,* ἐπιτηρητὴς, *April,* 1597, *to early in* 1599.]

Matthaios II[2]

Neophytos II[1], metropolitan of Athens.

Raphael II, moved in 1603 his residence from S. Demetrios to S. George (the Phanar).

Neophytos II[2], deposed and banished to Rhodes.

Cyrillos I[1], Lucaris, Patriarch of Alexandria.

Timotheos II, poisoned.

Cyrillos I[2]

Gregorios IV, metropolitan of Amaseia, deposed and banished to Rhodes.

Anthimos II

Cyrillos I[3]

Isaac

Cyrillos I[4]

Cyrillos II[1], metropolitan of Berrhoia.

Athanasios III[1], Pantellarios, metropolitan of Thessalonica.

Cyrillos I[5]

Cyrillos II[2], Contares

Neophytos III

Cyrillos I[6]

Cyrillos II[3]

Parthenios I, Geron: deposed and banished to Cyprus; died of poison at Chios.

Parthenios II[1], metropolitan of Adrianople, deposed and banished.

Ioannikios II[1], metropolitan of Heracleia, Lindios.

Parthenios II[2], Oxys: murdered at the instigation of the Princes of Wallachia and Moldavia.

Ioannikios II[2]

Cyrillos III[1], Spanos: metropolitan of Tornovo.

Athanasios III[3], fifteen days, resigned and died in Russia.

Paisios I[1]

Ioannikios II[3]

Cyrillos III[2], deposed and banished to Cyprus.

Paisios I[2]
Ioannikios II[4]
Parthenios III
(200)   Gabriel II, twelve days.
Thcophanes II, three days.
Parthenios IV[1], Mogilalos
Dionysios III, Bardalis
Parthenios IV[2]
Clemes, a few days, deposed and banished.
Methodios III, Morones, resigned and died at Venice.
Parthenios IV[3], six months, deposed and banished to Cyprus.
Dionysios IV[1], Muselimes.   Synod of Jerusalem, 1672.
Gerasimos II
Parthenios IV[4]
Dionysios IV[2].   First Orthodox church built in London, 1677.
Athanasios IV, a week, deposed and banished.
Iacobos[1]
Dionysios IV[3]
Parthenios IV[5], seven months.
Iacobos[2]
Dionysios IV[4]
Iacobos[3], four months.
Callinicos II[1], Acarnan, nine months.
Neophytos IV, five months.
Callinicos II[2]
Dionysios IV[5], seven months, deposed and died at Bucarest.
Callinicos II[3]
Gabriel III
Neophytos IV, election not confirmed by the Porte.
Cyprianos[1], deposed and banished to M. Athos.
Athanasios V
Cyrillos IV
Cyprianos[2], three months.
Cosmas III
Hieremias III[1]
Callinicos III, died of joy on hearing of his election, Nov. 19, 1726.
Paisios II[1], Kynmurji-oghlu, deposed and banished to Cyprus.
Hieremias III[2], six months.

Serapheim I, a year, deposed and banished to Lemnos.

Neophytos VI[1]

Paisios II[2]

Neophytos VI[2], ten months, deposed and banished to Patmos.

Paisios II[3]

Cyrillos V[1], Caracalos

Paisios II[4]

Cyrillos V[2], deposed and banished to M. Sinai.

Callinicos IV, deposed and banished to M. Sinai.

Serapheim II, an Imperial Rescript of 1759 decreed that the expenses of the election, reckoned at 120,000 francs, should be met by the new Patriarch.

Ioannikios III, Carajas, deposed and banished to M. Athos.

Samuel[1], Khanjeris, deposed and banished to M. Athos.

Meletios II, six months, resigned and died in penury at Mitylene.

Theodosios II, Maridakes, deposed and banished to Chalcis.

Samuel[2], 13 months, deposed.

Sophronios II, Patriarch of Jerusalem.

Gabriel IV

Procopios, deposed and banished to M. Athos.

Neophytos VII[1], deposed and banished to Rhodes.

Gerasimos III, a Cypriot.

Gregorios V[1], deposed and banished to M. Athos.

Neophytos VII[2], deposed and banished to M. Athos.

Callinicos V[1]

Gregorios V[2], deposed and banished to M. Athos.

Callinicos V[2], eight months.

Hieremias IV

Cyrillos VI, Serbetoghlu

Gregorios V[3], on Easter Day, April 22, 1821, hanged over the gate of the Patriarchate.

Eugenios II

Anthimos III, deposed and banished to Caisareia.

Chrysanthos, deposed and banished to Caisareia.

Agathangelos, deposed and banished to Caisareia.

Constantios I, archbishop of Sinai.

Constantios II

Gregorios VI[1], Khatti-Sherif of Gülkhane, Nov. 2, 1839.

Anthimos IV[1], Bambakes

Anthimos V

Germanos IV[1]

Meletios III, seven months.

Anthimos VI[1], Ioannides

Anthimos IV[2]

Germanos IV[2], nine months.

(**250**) Anthimos VI[2]

Cyrillos VII, Khatti-Humayun, Feb. 18, 1856.

Ioakeim II[2], Kokkodes

Sophronios III, deposed 1866, elected 1870 Patriarch of Alexandria.

Gregorios VI[2]

Anthimos VI[3]

Ioakeim II[2]

Ioakeim III[1], born 1834, metropolitan of Thessalonica ; resigned
    1884.

Neophytos VIII, deposed Oct. 1894.

Anthimos VII, deposed Feb. 1897.

(**257**) Constantinos V, deposed 1901.

Ioakeim III[2], re-elected June, 1901. *εἰς πολλὰ ἔτη.*

C. D. C.

INTRODUCTION I

THE rise of the see of Constantinople, the 'Great Church of Christ,' is the most curious development in the history of Eastern Christendom. For many centuries the patriarchs of New Rome have been the first bishops in the East. Though they never succeeded in the claim to universal jurisdiction over the whole Orthodox Church that they have at various times advanced, though, during the last century especially, the limits of their once enormous patriarchate have been ruthlessly driven back, nevertheless since the fifth century and still at the present time the Patriarch of New Rome fills a place in the great Christian body whose importance makes it second only to that of the Pope of Old Rome. To be an orthodox Christian one must accept the orthodox faith. That is the first criterion. And then as a second and visible bond of union all Greeks at any rate, and probably most Arabs and Slavs, would add that one must be in communion with the œcumenical patriarch. The Bulgars are entirely orthodox in faith, but are excommunicate from the see of Constantinople; a rather less acute form of the same state was until lately the misfortune of the Church of Antioch. And the great number of orthodox Christians would deny a share in their name to Bulgars and Antiochenes for this reason only. Since, then, these patriarchs are now and have so long been the centre of unity to the hundred millions of Christians who make up the great Orthodox Church, one might be tempted to think that their position is an essential element of its constitution, and to imagine that, since the days of the first general councils New Rome has been as much the leading Church of the East as Old Rome of the West. One might be tempted to conceive the Orthodox as the subjects of the œcumenical patriarch, just as Roman Catholics are the subjects of the pope This would be a mistake. The advance of the see of Constantinople is the latest development in the history of the hierarchy. The Byzantine patriarch is the youngest of the five. His see evolved from the smallest of local dioceses at the end of the fourth and during the fifth centuries. And now his jurisdiction, that at one time grew into something like that of his old rival the pope, has steadily retreated till he finds himself back not very far from the point at which his predecessors began their career of gradual advance. And the overwhelming majority of the Orthodox, although they still insist on communion with him, indignantly deny that he has any rights over them. Though they still give him a place of honour as the first bishop of their Church, the other orthodox patriarchs and still more the synods of national churches show a steadily growing jealousy of his assumption and a defiant insistence on their equality with him. An outline of the story of what may perhaps be called the rise and fall of the see of Constantinople will form the natural introduction to the list of its bishops.

We first hear of a bishop of Byzantium at the time of the first General Council (Nicaea, 325). At that time Metrophanes (315—325) ruled what was only a small local see under the metropolitan of Thrace at Herakleia. Long afterwards his successors claimed St Andrew the Apostle as the founder of their see. This legend does not begin till about the ninth century, after Constantinople had become a mighty patriarchate. There was always a feeling that the chief sees should be those founded by apostles; the other patriarchates—Rome, Alexandria, Antioch and Jerusalem—were apostolic sees (Alexandria claimed St Peter as her founder too), and now that Constantinople was to be the equal of the others, indeed the second see of all, an apostolic founder had to be found for her too. The legend of St Andrew at Constantinople first occurs in a ninth century forgery attributed to one Dorotheos, bishop of Tyre and a martyr under Diocletian. St Andrew's successor is said to be the Stachys mentioned in Rom. xvi. 9; and then follow Onesimos and twenty-two other mythical bishops, till we come to a real person, Metrophanes I. The reason why St Andrew was chosen is the tradition that he went to the North and preached in Scythia, Epirus and Thrace. No one now takes this first line of Byzantine bishops seriously. Their names are interesting as one more example of an attempt to connect what afterwards became a great see with an apostle. Before the ninth century one of the commonest charges brought against the growing patriarchate was that it is not an apostolic see (e.g. Leo I. *Ep.* 104, *ad Marcianum*), and its defenders never think of denying the charge; they rather bring the question quite candidly to its real issue by answering that it is at any rate an imperial one. So the first historical predecessor of the œcumenical patriarch was Metrophanes I. And he was by no means an œcumenical patriarch. He was not even a metropolitan. His city at the time of the first Nicene synod was a place of no sort of importance, and he was the smallest of local bishops who obeyed the metropolitan of Herakleia. The council recognized as an 'ancient use' the rights of three chief sees only—*Rome*, *Alexandria* and *Antioch* (Can. 6). The title 'patriarch' (taken, of course, from the Old Testament as 'Levite' for deacon) only gradually became a technical one. It is the case of nearly all ecclesiastical titles. As late as the sixth century we still find any specially venerable bishop called a patriarch (Greg. Naz. *Orat.* 42, 43, *Acta SS.* Febr. III. 742, where Celidonius of Besançon is called 'the venerable patriarch'). But the thing itself was there, if not the special name. At the time of Nicæa I. there were three and only three bishops who stood above other metropolitans and ruled over vast provinces, the bishops first of Rome, then of Alexandria and thirdly of Antioch. It should be noticed that conservative people, and especially the Western Church, for centuries resented the addition of the two new patriarchates— *Jerusalem* and *Constantinople*—to these three, and still clung to the ideal of three chief Churches only. Constantinople eventually displaced Alexandria and Antioch to the third and fourth places: they both refused to accept that position for a long time. Alexandria constantly in the fifth and sixth centuries asserts her right as the 'second throne,' and Antioch demands to be recognized as third. The Roman Church especially maintained the older theory; she did not formally recognize Constantinople as a patriarchate at all till the ninth century, when she accepted the 21st Canon of Constantinople IV. (869) that establishes the order of five patriarchates, with Constantinople as the second and Jerusalem as the last. Dioscur of Alexandria (444—451) bitterly resented the lowered place given to his see. St Leo I. of Rome (440—461) writes: 'Let the great Churches keep their dignity according to the Canons, that is Alexandria and Antioch' (*Ep. ad Rufin. Thess.*, Le Quien, *Or. Christ.* I. 18), and he constantly appeals to the sixth Canon of Nicæa against later innovations (Ep. 104, *ad Marc.*). He says: 'The dignity of the Alexandrine see must not perish' and 'the Antiochene Church should remain in the order arranged by the Fathers, so that having been put in the third place it should never be reduced to a lower one' (Ep. 106, *ad Anatolium*). St Gregory I. (590—604) still cherished the older ideal of the three patriarchates, and as late as the eleventh century St Leo IX. (1045—1054) writes to Peter III. of Antioch that 'Antioch must keep the third place' (Will, *Acta et scripta de controversiis eccl. graecae et latinae*, Leipzig, 1861, p. 168). However, in spite of all opposition the bishops of Constantinople succeeded, first in being recognized as patriarchs and eventually as taking the second place, after Rome but before Alexandria. It was purely an accident of secular politics that made this possible. The first general council had not even mentioned the insignificant little diocese of Byzantium. But by the time the second council met (Constantinople I., 381) a great change had happened. Constantine in 330 dedicated his new capital 'amid the nakedness of almost all other cities'

(St Jerome, *Chron.* A.D. 332). He moved the seat of his government thither, stripped Old Rome and ransacked the Empire to adorn it, and built up what became the most gorgeous city of the world. So the bishop of Byzantium found himself in a sense the special bishop of Cæsar. He at once obtained an honoured place at court, he had the ear of the emperor, he was always at hand to transact any business between other bishops and the government. Politically and civilly New Rome was to be in every way equal to Old Rome, and since the fourth century there was a strong tendency to imitate civil arrangements in ecclesiastical affairs. Could the prelate whose place had suddenly become so supremely important remain a small local ordinary under a metropolitan? And always the emperors favoured the ambition of their court bishops; the greater the importance of their capital in the Church, as well as in the State, the more would the loyalty of their subjects be riveted to the central government. So we find that the advance of the Byzantine see is always as desirable an object to the emperor as to his bishop. The advance came quickly now. But we may notice that at every step there is no sort of concealment as to its motive. No one in those days thought of claiming any other reason for the high place given to the bishop except the fact that the imperial court sat in his city. There was no pretence of an apostolic foundation, no question of St Andrew, no claim to a glorious past, no record of martyrs, doctors nor saints who had adorned the see of this new city; she had taken no part in spreading the faith, had been of no importance to anyone till Constantine noticed what a splendid site the Bosphorus and Golden Horn offer.

This little bishop was *parvenu* of the *parvenus*; he knew it and everyone knew it. His one argument—and for four centuries he was never tired of repeating it—was that he was the emperor's bishop, his see was New Rome. New Rome was civilly equal to Old Rome, so why should he not be as great, or nearly as great, as that distant patriarch now left alone where the weeds choked ruined gates by the Tiber? Now that the splendour of Cæsar and his court have gone to that dim world where linger the ghosts of Pharaoh and Cyrus we realize how weak was the foundation of this claim from the beginning. The Turk has answered the new patriarch's arguments very effectively. And to-day he affects an attitude of conservatism, and in his endless quarrels with the independent Orthodox Churches he talks about ancient rights. He has no ancient rights. The ancient rights are those of his betters at Rome, Alexandria and Antioch. His high place is founded on an accident of politics, and if his argument were carried out consistently he would have had to step down in 1453 and the chief bishops of Christendom would now be those of Paris, London and New York. We must go back to 381 and trace the steps of his progress. The first Council of Constantinople was a small assembly of only 150 eastern bishops. No Latins were present, the Roman Church was not represented. Its third canon ordains that: 'The bishop of Constantinople shall have the primacy of honour (τὰ πρεσβεῖα τῆς τιμῆς) after the bishop of Rome, because that city is New Rome.' This does not yet mean a patriarchate. There is no question of extra-diocesan jurisdiction. He is to have an honorary place after the pope because his city has become politically New Rome. The Churches of Rome and Alexandria definitely refused to accept this canon. The popes in accepting the Creed of Constantinople I. always rejected its canons and specially rejected this third canon. Two hundred years later Gregory I. says, 'The Roman Church neither acknowledges nor receives the canons of that synod, she accepts the said synod in what it defined against Macedonius' (the additions to the Nicene Creed, *Ep.* VII. 34); and when Gratian put the canon into the Roman canon law in the twelfth century the papal correctors added to it a note to the effect that the Roman Church did not acknowledge it. The canon and the note still stand in the *Corpus juris* (dist. XXII. c. 3), a memory of the opposition with which Old Rome met the first beginning of the advance of New Rome. The third general council did not affect this advance, although during the whole fourth century there are endless cases of bishops of Constantinople, defended by the emperor, usurping rights in other provinces—usurpations that are always indignantly opposed by the lawful primates. Such usurpations, and the indignant oppositions, fill up the history of the Eastern Church down to our own time. It was the fourth general council (Chalcedon in 451) that finally assured the position of the imperial bishops. Its 28th canon is the vital point in all this story. The canon—very long and confused in its form—defines that 'the most holy Church of Constantinople the New Rome' shall have a primacy next after Old Rome. Of course the invariable reason is given: 'the city honoured because of her rule and her Senate shall enjoy a like primacy to that of the elder Imperial Rome and shall be mighty in Church affairs just as she is and shall be second after her." The canon gives authority over Asia (the Roman province, of course— Asia Minor) and Thrace to Constantinople and so builds up a new patriarchate. Older and infinitely more venerable sees, Herakleia, the ancient metropolis, Caesarea in Cappadocia, that had converted all Armenia, Ephesus where the apostle whom our Lord loved had sat—they must all step down, because Constantinople is honoured for her rule and her senate. The Roman legates (Lucentius, Paschasius and Boniface) were away at the fifteenth session when this canon was drawn up. When they arrive later and hear what has been done in their absence they are very angry, and a heated discussion takes place in which they appeal to the sixth canon of Nicæa. The council sent an exceptionally respectful letter to Pope Leo I. (440—461) asking him to confirm their acts (*Ep. Conc. Chal. ad Leonem*, among St Leo's letters, No. 98). He confirms the others, but rejects the twenty-eighth categorically. ' He who seeks undue honours,' he says, 'loses his real ones. Let it be enough for the said Bishop' (Anatolios of Constantinople) 'that by the help of your' (Marcian's) 'piety and by the consent of my favour he has got the bishopric of so great a city. Let him not despise a royal see because he can never make it an apostolic one' (no one had dreamed of the St Andrew legend then); 'nor should he by any means hope to become greater by offending others.' He also appeals to canon 6 of Nicaea against the proposed arrangement (*Ep.* 104). So the 28th canon of Chalcedon, too, was never admitted at Rome. The Illyrian and various other bishops had already refused to sign it. Notwithstanding this opposition the new patriarch con-

tinued to prosper. The Council of Chalcedon had made
the see of Jerusalem into a patriarchate as well, giving it
the fifth place. But all the eastern rivals go down in
importance at this time. Alexandria, Antioch and
Jerusalem were overrun with Monophysites; nearly all
Syria and Egypt fell away into that heresy, so that the
orthodox patriarchs had scarcely any flocks. Then came
Islam and swept away whatever power they still had.
Meanwhile Cæsar was always the friend of his own
bishop. Leo III., the Isaurian (717—741), filched his
own fatherland, Isauria, from Antioch and gave it to
Constantinople; from the seventh to the ninth centuries
the emperors continually affect to separate Illyricum
from the Roman patriarchate and to add it to that of
their own bishop. Since Justinian conquered back Italy
(554) they claim Greater Greece (Southern Italy, Calabria, Apulia, Sicily) for their patriarch too, till the
Norman Conquest (1060—1091) puts an end to any
hope of asserting such a claim. It is the patriarch of
Constantinople who has the right of crowning the
emperor; and the patriarch John IV., the Faster
(Νηστευτής, 582—595), assumes the vaguely splendid
title of 'Œcumenical Patriarch.' The new kingdom
of the Bulgars forms a source of angry dispute between
Rome and Constantinople, till just after the great schism
the œcumenical patriarch wins them all to his side,
little thinking how much trouble the children of these
same Bulgars will some day give to his successors.
Photios (857—867, 878—886) and Michael Kerularios
(Michael I., 1043—1058) saw the great schism between
East and West. Meanwhile the conversion of the
Russians (988) added an enormous territory to what

was already the greatest of the Eastern patriarchates.

The Turkish conquest of Constantinople (1453), strangely enough, added still more to the power of its patriarchs. True to their unchanging attitude the Mohammedans accepted each religious communion as a civil body. The Rayahs were grouped according to their Churches. The greatest of these bodies was, and is, the Orthodox Church, with the name ' Roman nation' (rum millet), strange survival of the dead empire. And the recognized civil head of this Roman nation is the œcumenical patriarch. So he now has civil jurisdiction over all orthodox Rayahs in the Turkisk empire, over the other patriarchs and their subjects and over the autocephalous Cypriotes as well as over the faithful of his own patriarchate. No orthodox Christian can approach the Porte except through his court at the Phanar. And the Phanar continually tries to use this civil jurisdiction for ecclesiastical purposes.

We have now come to the height of our patriarch's power. He rules over a vast territory second only to that of the Roman patriarchate. All Turkey in Europe, all Asia Minor, and Russia to the Polish frontier and the White Sea, obey the great lord who rules by the old lighthouse on the Golden Horn. And he is politically and civilly the overlord of Orthodox Egypt, Syria, Palestine and Cyprus as well. So for one short period, from 1453 to 1589, he was not a bad imitation of the real pope. But his glory did not last, and from this point to the present time his power has gone down almost as fast as it went up in the fourth and fifth centuries. The first blow was the independence of

Russia. In 1589 the czar, Feodor Ivanovich, made his Church into an autocephalous patriarchate (under Moscow), and in 1721 Peter the Great changed its government into that of a 'Holy directing Synod.' Both the independence and the synod have been imitated by most Orthodox Churches since. Jeremias II. of Constantinople (1572—1579, 1580—1584, 1586—1595) took money as the price of acknowledging the Russian Holy Synod as his 'sister in Christ.' It was all he could do. His protector the Sultan had no power in Russia, and if he had made difficulties he would not have prevented what happened and he would have lost the bribe. Since then the œcumenical patriarch has no kind of jurisdiction in Russia ; even the holy chrism is prepared at Petersburg. In two small cases the Phanar gained a point since it lost Russia. Through the unholy alliance with the Turkish government that had become its fixed policy, it succeeded in crushing the independent Servian Church of Ipek in 1765 and the Bulgarian Church of Achrida (Ochrida in Macedonia) in 1767. The little Roumanian Church of Tirnovo had been forced to submit to Constantinople as soon as the Turks conquered that city (1393). In these three cases, then, the Phanar again spread the boundaries of its jurisdiction. Otherwise it steadily retreats. In every case in which a Balkan State has thrown off the authority of the Porte, its Church has at once thrown off the authority of the Phanar. These two powers had been too closely allied for the new independent government to allow its subjects to obey either of them. The process is always the same. One of the first laws of the new constitution is to declare that the national

Church is entirely orthodox, that it accepts all canons, decrees and declarations of the Seven Holy Synods, that it remains in communion with the œcumenical throne and with all other Orthodox Churches of Christ; but that it is an entirely autocephalous Church, acknowledging no head but Christ. A Holy Synod is then set up on the Russian model, by which the theory 'no head but Christ' always works out as unmitigated Erastianism. The patriarch on the other hand is always filled with indignation; he always protests vehemently, generally begins by excommunicating the whole of the new Church, and (except in the Bulgarian case) Russia always makes him eventually withdraw his decree and recognize yet another sister in Christ.

In 1833 the first Greek parliament at Nauplion declared the Greek Church independent; Anthimos IV. of Constantinople first refused to acknowledge it at all and then in 1850 published his famous *Tomos*, allowing some measure of self-government. The Greek Church refused to take any notice of the *Tomos*, and eventually Anthimos had to give way altogether. In 1866 the cession of the Ionian Isles, and in 1881 the addition of Thessaly and part of Epirus to the kingdom of Greece, enlarged the territory of the Greek Church and further reduced the patriarchate. In 1870 the Bulgars founded an independent national Church. This is by far the worst trouble of all. They have set up an Exarch in Constantinople and he claims jurisdiction over all Bulgars, wherever they may live. The Bulgarian Church is recognized by Russia, excommunicate and most vehemently denounced by the patriarch. The inevitable moment in which the Phanar will have to give way and welcome this sister too has not yet come. The Serbs set up their Church in 1879, the Vlachs in 1885— both establishments led to disputes that still distress the Orthodox Church. The Austrian occupation of lands inhabited by orthodox Christians has led to the establishment of independent Churches at Carlovitz in 1765, at Hermannstadt (Nagy-Szeben) in 1864, at Czernovitz in 1873 and of a practically independent one in Hercegovina and Bosnia since 1880. The diminishing power of the œcumenical patriarch is further shown by the resistance, always more and more uncompromising, shown when he tries to interfere in the affairs of the other patriarchates and autocephalous Churches. In 1866 Sophronios III. of Constantinople wanted to judge a case at the monastery of Mount Sinai. Immediately the Patriarch of Jerusalem summoned a synod and indignantly refused to acknowledge his ' anti-canonical interference and his foreign and unknown authority.' The Church of Greece since its establishment has had many opportunities of resisting the patriarch's foreign authority. She has not failed to use each of them. The see of Antioch still bears the excommunication proclaimed against her late Patriarch Meletios († Feb. 8, 1906) rather than allow the Phanar to interfere in her affairs. The patriarch of Alexandria (Photios) has sent away the legate whom the Phanar wished to keep at his court. The Church of Cyprus, now for nearly nine years in the throes of a quarrel that disturbs and scandalizes the whole orthodox world, has appealed to every sort of person—including the British Colonial Office—to come and help her out of her trouble. From only one will she hear of no interference. Every time the Phanar volunteers a little well-meant advice it is told sharply that it has no authority in Cyprus; the Council of Ephesus in 431 settled all that, and, in short, will his All-Holiness of Constantinople mind his own business?

The diminished authority of the œcumenical throne now covers Turkey in Europe (that is, Thrace, Macedonia and part of Epirus) and Asia Minor only. And in Macedonia its rights are denied by the Bulgars; and both Serbs and Vlachs are on the point of setting up independent Churches here too.

The patriarch however takes precedence of all other orthodox bishops. His title is 'Archbishop of Constantinople, New Rome and Œcumenical Patriarch' ('Ο παναγιώτατος, ὁ θειότατος, ὁ σοφώτατος κύριος, ὁ Ἀρχιεπίσκοπος Κωνσταντινουπόλεως, Νέας Ῥώμης καὶ οἰκουμενικός Πατριάρχης). He is addressed as 'Your most divine All-Holiness' ('Η Ὑμετέρα Θειοτάτη Παναγιότης). To assist him in his rule he has two tribunals, a synod for purely ecclesiastical affairs and a 'mixed national council (μικτὸν ἐθνικὸν συμβούλιον)' for affairs that are partly ecclesiastical and partly secular.

Since 1860 the patriarchs are elected—nominally for life—in this way: a committee of the metropolitan bishops present in Constantinople, with certain laymen and representatives of twenty-six provincial bishops, meets not less than forty days after the vacancy and submits to the Porte the names of all for whom their votes have been recorded. From this list the Sultan may strike out not more than three names. Out of the corrected list the mixed council chooses three; and the synod finally elects one of the three. But the candidate who has steered his way through all these trials is not yet appointed. He must be confirmed by the Sultan, who may even now reject him. The patriarch-elect at last receives a *berat*, that is a form of appointment by the Sultan, in which his civil and ecclesiastical rights are exactly defined, is solemnly invested by the Great Wazīr in the Sultan's name, pays certain visits of ceremony to various Turkish officials and is finally enthroned in the Church of St George in the Phanar. The enthronement is performed by the metropolitan of Herakleia (last shadow of his old jurisdiction over Byzantium) after the Turkish officer has read out the berat. The patriarchs are still obliged to pay heavy bribes for their berat. Their dress is the same as that of other orthodox bishops, except that the veil of the patriarch's *Kalemaukion* is often violet. As arms on their seal they bear a spread eagle imperially crowned.

The first glance at the list will reveal what is the greatest abuse of the œcumenical throne, namely the enormous number of its occupants and the short length of their reigns. Even before 1453, and very much more since the Turk has reigned here, the patriarchs are deposed incessantly. Sometimes it is the government, more often the endless strife of parties in the Church, that brings about this everlasting course of deposition, resignation and reappointment. The thing has reached incredible proportions. Scarcely any patriarch has reigned for more than two or three years before he has been forced to resign. Between 1625 and 1700, for instance, there were fifty patriarchs, an average of eighteen months' reign for each. But when a patriarch is deposed he does not take final leave of the œcumenical throne. He always has a party on his side and that party immediately begins intriguing for his restoration. Generally there are three or four candidates who go backwards and forwards at short intervals; each is deposed and one of his rivals reappointed. All the Phanariote Greeks then naturally swerve round to the opposition and move heaven and earth to have the present occupier removed and one of the ex-patriarchs re-elected. They quarrel and criticize all the reigning patriarch's actions, the metropolitans refuse to work with him; everyone besieges the Turkish Minister of Police with petitions till he is made to resign. Then one of his old rivals is appointed again and everyone begins trying to oust him. So the proceeding goes on round and round. And the Porte gets its bribe for each new berat. Some patriarchs have had as many as five tenures at intervals (Cyril Lukaris had six). There are always three or four ex-patriarchs waiting in angry retirement at Athos or Chalki for a chance of reappointment; so unless one has just seen the current number of the Ἐκκλησιαστικὴ Ἀλήθεια it is never safe to say certainly which is the patriarch and which an ex-patriarch.

The reigning patriarch, Joakim III., had already occupied the see from 1878 to 1884. When Constantine V. fell in 1901 he was re-elected and has reigned for nearly seven years—an almost unique record. There are now three ex-patriarchs, each with a party angrily demanding its favourite's reappointment, Neophytos VIII., Anthimos VII. and Constantine V. Anthimos VII. has made himself specially conspicuous as a critic of his successor's actions. He constantly writes to point out how much better he managed things during his reign (1884—1897) and how much better he would manage them again if he had the chance. In 1905 nine metropolitans (led by Joakim of Ephesus and Prokopios of Durazzo) proceeded to depose Joakim III. They telegraphed to Petersburg, Athens, Belgrade and Bucharest that the patriarchal see was again vacant. Joakim of Ephesus was the popular candidate for the succession. This was all natural and right, and would have four ex-patriarchs instead of three—till they had ousted the Ephesian. Only this time they counted without their host. The Porte means—or meant then—to keep Joakim III.; and the only thing that really ever matters in the Byzantine patriarchate is what the Sultan decides. So these metropolitans were severely lectured by Abdurrahmān Pasha, the Minister of Police; Joakim was lectured too and his duty as patriarch was plainly explained to him, but he kept his place, and for once the Porte threw away a chance of selling another berat. Abdurrahmān seems to be the normally appointed person to point out the laws of the Orthodox Church to its metropolitan, and there is an inimitable touch of irony in the date, ' 18 Rabi'al-awwal, 1323,' for instance, that he puts at the end of his canonical epistles to the patriarch.

The list that follows contains an astonishingly small number of great names. One is always reminded that but for the protection of the emperor and then of the Sultan the see of Constantinople has no claim to dignity. Alexandria, Antioch and Jerusalem have all incomparably more honourable memories. At Constantinople only two really great patriarchs have brought honour to their see—St John Chrysostom (398—404) and Photios (857—867, 878—886). Nestorios (428—431), the Monotheletes Sergios I. (610—638), Pyrrhos I. (638—641) and Paul II. (641—652), and especially poor Cyril Lukaris (1621 at six intervals to 1638), made a certain name for themselves, but their successors would hardly glory in their memory. On the other hand, in a long list that tells of little but time-serving, grovelling subjection to the Turk and ludicrous intrigue, there are some names that stand out as those of men who stood boldly for the cause of Christ against the unbaptized tyrant to whom they owed their place ; and there are even martyrs who have left to this see a more real glory than that of the mythical apostle-patriarch, St Andrew. Isidore II. (1456—1463) was murdered for refusing to allow a Christian woman to become the second wife of a Mohammedan, Maximos III. (1476—1482) was mutilated for the same cause and Gregory V. (1797 at three intervals to 1822) was barbarously hanged on Easter-day 1821 as a revenge because his countrymen were defeating his master.

And lastly, of the reigning patriarch, Joakim III., there is nothing to say but what is very good. He began his second reign by sending an Encyclical to the other Orthodox Churches in which he proposed certain very excellent reforms (for instance that of their Calendar), wished to arrange a better understanding between the sixteen independent bodies that make up their communion and expressed his pious hope for the re-union of Christendom. Pity that their never-ending jealousies made those of these Churches that answered at all do so in the most unfriendly way. But of Joakim himself one hears everything that is edifying. He is evidently really concerned about the scandals that disgrace the Orthodox name—the affairs of Bulgaria, Antioch, Cyprus and so on— and he has shown himself in every way a wise, temperate and godly bishop. So one may end this note by expressing a very sincere hope that he may be allowed to go on ruling the Great Church of Christ for many years still before the inevitable deposition comes.

And for the sake of removing the crying scandal of these constant changes in the patriarchate, as well as for the sympathy we all feel for his character, the Western outsider will join very heartily in the greeting with which he was received at his enthronement : ᾿Ιωακεὶμ ἄξιος—εἰς πολλὰ ἔτη.

ADRIAN FORTESCUE.

INTRODUCTION II

The population of the Roman Empire was divided into groups by the system of provinces, and to this grouping the Churches of Christendom seem to have accommodated themselves almost, if not quite, from the very beginning. Thus, for instance, the Churches of Syria, from very early days indeed, formed one group, the head of which was the Church of Antioch, the chief city of the province. The Church of Antioch was indeed the 'metropolis,' of which the other Syrian churches, for the most part at any rate, were 'colonies'; but Antioch had been selected as the missionary centre, we may be sure, on account of its being the provincial capital. Again, the Churches of Asia formed a group, in which the lead belonged to the Church of Ephesus, the Churches of Macedonia (Eastern Illyricum) another group, in which the chief place was taken by the Church of Thessalonica, and yet another group was that of the Achaian Churches, centreing about the Church of Corinth. Other examples of Churches whose grouping corresponded with provincial divisions of the Empire were those of Cyprus, Egypt, and Africa.

This correspondence of grouping between the Church and the Empire is more easily exemplified from the regions to the east of the Adriatic than from those to the west of it. One reason, no doubt, is the fact that, even down to Bishop Jewel's famous limit of 'Catholic Antiquity,' viz. the end of the sixth century, the history of Christendom is the history of the Eastern, much more than of the Western, Churches. Still, the correspondence does not cease when we pass from Greece and the East to Italy and the West. Carthage and Africa have been already mentioned, and in connection with that region of the Roman Empire it should be noticed that just as Carthage and the African provinces were, if anything, more Latin than Rome and Latium itself, in the earliest period of Christian history, so it was in Carthage and Africa, not in Rome, that the forefathers of Latin Christianity arose—Tertullian, Cyprian, Augustine[1]. Again, in the Eastern half of the Empire, great and famous cities were numerous—Alexandria, Antioch, Tarsus, the Cappadocian Cæsarea, Ephesus, Thessalonica, Corinth—and so were notable Christian bishoprics. In the Western half, Rome, Milan and Carthage for a considerable time threw all the rest very much into the shade. Lyon, of course, was a considerable city—and we find one of the most ancient Churches of the West founded there, and undergoing persecution in the year 177. But Lyon was a new creation. The Roman Empire had called it into being, whereas the great cities of the East had a history reaching back to times long before the Roman Empire had begun to be. Very naturally, then, in the grouping of Christendom, the

---

[1] The 'Old Latin' version of the New Testament was produced in the province of Africa, in the second century. See Westcott, *Canon of the New Testament*, I. iii. 3.

whole West, speaking generally, was regarded as one group, with Rome as its head and centre. Even those who made a separate group or province of the African Churches would hardly assign anything less extensive than Italy and the Italian islands, Spain and Gaul, and Britain, as the province of the Roman See. The care of all the churches in those countries would be regarded by all as properly coming upon and assumed by the bishop of Rome.

Among the cities of the East, two stood far out and above the rest, for size, and wealth, and all that goes to make urban greatness—Alexandria, to wit, and Antioch. Speaking generally with regard to the first 300 years of the Christian era, one would say that next in the scale of greatness and importance came the following three— Cæsarea in Cappadocia, Ephesus and Thessalonica ; three most important points, one may observe, on the chief line of communication between Rome and the Euphrates frontier of the Empire. In the West, Rome shone with absolutely unique glory. Lyon, Milan, Ravenna, even Carthage itself, which after all had been resuscitated by the grace of her quondam rival—these were nothing accounted of in comparison with Rome.

The Emperor Diocletian (A.D. 284—305) made considerable modifications in the provincial system of the Roman Empire, distributing all the provinces into 12 'dioceses' or groups of provinces. During the fourth century other changes were made, and in A.D. 400 the number of dioceses had been increased from 12 to 13[1]. A profoundly important change in the structure of the

---

[1] See Professor Bury's edition of Gibbon, *Decline and Fall*, vol. II. p. 541 f.

Empire was effected by the foundation of a new imperial capital, Constantinople, the 'Encænia' of which were celebrated on the 11th of May, A.D. 330[1].

At the time of the great Council of Nicæa, the building of 'the city of Constantine, New Rome,' had only just been begun. The greatest cities of Christendom, in A.D. 325, are also the greatest cities of the Empire—Rome, Alexandria, Antioch. The Nicene Council, representative of all Christendom, ordered in the sixth of the twenty canons which it passed, that the ancient customs should prevail, whereby the bishop of Alexandria exercised authority over the churches in Egypt, Libya, and Pentapolis ('the parts of Libya about Cyrene'), and similar authority over a wide area was exercised, in the West by the bishop of Rome, in the East by the bishop of Antioch[2]. The limits of authority and jurisdiction are not specified in the case either of Rome or of Antioch, so that the canon, taken by itself, is evidence for no more than the fact that the bishop, in each of these cities, had a 'province' in which he was the chief pastor. Other churches, besides those of Rome, Alexandria and Antioch, had prerogatives and privileges—πρεσβεῖα—which were to be maintained. The Canon goes on to speak of the necessity incumbent

---

[1] Gibbon, *Decline and Fall*, II. p. 157, note 65 (Bury's edition). Ὡρολόγιον τὸ Μέγα, p. 310, where the 11th of May is called τὰ γενέθλια ἤτοι τὰ ἐγκαίνια τῆς Κωσταντινουπόλεως. The Orthodox Church placed the city under the especial favour and protection of the Blessed Virgin Mary.

[2] Concil. Nicæn. Can. VI. τὰ ἀρχαῖα ἔθη κρατείτω, τὰ ἐν Αἰγύπτῳ καὶ Λιβύῃ καὶ Πενταπόλει, ὥστε τὸν ἐν Ἀλεξανδρείᾳ ἐπίσκοπον πάντων τούτων ἔχειν τὴν ἐξουσίαν, ἐπειδὴ καὶ τῷ ἐν Ῥώμῃ ἐπισκόπῳ τοῦτο σύνηθές ἐστιν. ὁμοίως δὲ καὶ κατὰ τὴν Ἀντιόχειαν, καὶ ἐν ταῖς ἄλλαις ἐπαρχίαις, τὰ πρεσβεῖα σώζεσθαι ταῖς ἐκκλησίαις.

on every bishop of obtaining his metropolitan's consent to his election and consecration. 'If any be made a bishop, without consent of his metropolitan, this great Synod has determined that such person ought not to be bishop[1].' This ruling finds illustration in the ninth Canon of the Council of Antioch, A.D. 341, according to which 'the bishop presiding in the metropolis ought to know the bishops of his province, and undertake the care of the whole province, because all, who have any business, congregate in the metropolis[2].' Without the metropolitan's cognizance, the bishops of a province ought not to take any action. This, it is asserted, was 'the rule of our fathers, established of old.' Each bishop had his distinct rights and duties, within the limits of his παροικία, or district; beyond those limits he could only act in concert with his metropolitan, and the metropolitan, in turn, must not act without the co-operation of his comprovincials.

The words 'metropolis' and 'province' were taken over by the Church from the official vocabulary of the Empire. 'Metropolis' in the sense of a 'capital' city or

---

[1] *Ibid.*, καθόλου δὲ πρόδηλον ἐκεῖνο, ὅτι εἴ τις χωρὶς γνώμης τοῦ μητροπολίτου γένοιτο ἐπίσκοπος, τὸν τοιοῦτον ἡ μεγάλη σύνοδος ὥρισε μὴ δεῖν εἶναι ἐπίσκοπον. ἐὰν μέντοι τῇ κοινῇ πάντων ψήφῳ, εὐλόγῳ οὔσῃ, καὶ κατὰ κανόνα ἐκκλησιαστικόν, δύο ἢ τρεῖς δι' οἰκείαν φιλονεικίαν ἀντιλέγωσι, κρατείτω ἡ τῶν πλειόνων ψῆφος.

[2] Concil. Antioch. Can. IX. τοὺς καθ' ἑκάστην ἐπισκόπους εἰδέναι χρὴ τὸν ἐν τῇ μητροπόλει προεστῶτα ἐπίσκοπον καὶ τὴν φροντίδα ἀναδέχεσθαι πάσης τῆς ἐπαρχίας, διὰ τὸ ἐν μητροπόλει πανταχόθεν συντρέχειν πάντας τοὺς πράγματα ἔχοντας, ὅθεν ἔδοξε καὶ τῇ τιμῇ προηγεῖσθαι αὐτόν, κατὰ τὸν ἀρχαῖον κρατήσαντα τῶν πατέρων ἡμῶν κανόνα, ἢ ταῦτα μόνα, ὅσα τῇ ἑκάστου ἐπιβάλλει παροικίᾳ καὶ ταῖς ὑπ' αὐτὴν χώραις. ἕκαστον γὰρ ἐπίσκοπον ἐξουσίαν ἔχειν τῆς ἑαυτοῦ παροικίας, διοικεῖν τε κατὰ τὴν ἑκάστῳ ἐπιβάλλουσαν εὐλάβειαν, καὶ πρόνοιαν ποιεῖσθαι πάσης τῆς χώρας τῆς ὑπὸ τὴν ἑαυτοῦ πόλιν, ὡς καὶ χειροτονεῖν πρεσβυτέρους καὶ διακόνους, καὶ μετὰ κρίσεως ἕκαστα διαλαμβάνειν,

town is met with as far back as the days of Xenophon[1]. In the Roman epoch it was a title of honour much sought after, and disputed over, by the cities of the province of Asia. The proper metropolis of Asia was Pergamus, the seat and centre of the government and of the κοινὸν or confederation of the provincial cities, but the title was claimed by, and allowed to, Ephesus, Smyrna, Sardis, and others besides[2]. As it happened, Ephesus was, in ecclesiastical relations, a true metropolis, the Churches of Asia being subordinate to it. There St Paul and St John had dwelt and laboured, and thence had the sound of the Gospel gone forth into all the province[3].

περαιτέρω δὲ μηδὲν πράττειν ἐπιχειρεῖν, δίχα τοῦ τῆς μητροπόλεως ἐπισκόπου, μηδὲ αὐτὸν ἄνευ τῆς τῶν λοιπῶν γνώμης. Compare the thirty-fourth of the so-called *Canons of the Holy Apostles*—τοὺς ἐπισκόπους ἑκάστου ἔθνους εἰδέναι χρὴ τὸν ἐν αὐτοῖς πρῶτον, καὶ ἡγεῖσθαι αὐτὸν ὡς κεφαλήν, καὶ μηδέν τι πράττειν περιττὸν ἄνευ τῆς ἐκείνου γνώμης, μόνα δὲ πράττειν ἕκαστον, ὅσα τῇ αὐτοῦ παροικίᾳ ἐπιβάλλει, καὶ ταῖς ὑπ᾽ αὐτὴν χώραις. ἀλλὰ μηδὲ ἐκεῖνος ἄνευ τῆς πάντων γνώμης ποιείτω τι. οὕτω γὰρ ὁμόνοια ἔσται, καὶ δοξασθήσεται ὁ Θεός, διὰ Κυρίου, ἐν Ἁγίῳ Πνεύματι, ὁ Πατὴρ καὶ ὁ Υἱὸς καὶ τὸ Ἅγιον Πνεῦμα. Also Concil. Nicæn. Can. IV. ἐπίσκοπον προσήκει μάλιστα μὲν ὑπὸ πάντων τῶν ἐν τῇ ἐπαρχίᾳ καθίστασθαι, εἰ δὲ δυσχερὲς εἴη τὸ τοιοῦτον… ἐξάπαντος τρεῖς ἐπὶ τὸ αὐτὸ συναγομένους, συμψήφων γενομένων καὶ τῶν ἀπόντων, καὶ συντιθεμένων διὰ γραμμάτων, τότε τὴν χειροτονίαν ποιεῖσθαι. τὸ δὲ κῦρος τῶν γινομένων δίδοσθαι καθ᾽ ἑκάστην ἐπαρχίαν τῷ μητροπολίτῃ.—Ἔθνος in the Apostolic Canon = provincia. See Ramsay, *Letters to the Seven Churches*, p. 229.

[1] Xenophon, *Anabasis* V. ii. 3, iv. 15.

[2] Mommsen, *The Provinces of the Roman Empire*, vol. I. pp. 329—330 (Eng. Transl.), Ramsay, *Letters to the Seven Churches*, pp. 227—230, 289—290.

[3] Acts xix., Rev. i. 9—11, Eusebius, *Hist. Eccl.* III. i. 23 (with citations from Irenæus and Clement) and v. 24 (letter of Polycrates, bishop of Ephesus, to Victor, bishop of Rome). In the last-mentioned passage Eusebius speaks of Polycrates as follows—τῶν δὲ ἐπὶ τῆς Ἀσίας ἐπισκόπων… ἡγεῖτο Πολυκράτης.

The bishops of Christendom, then, were grouped round metropolitans. In their turn, the metropolitans were subordinate to the bishops of the first-rate cities of the Empire. Thus the metropolitans in Spain, Gaul and Britain, and Italy, were subordinate to the bishop of Rome, who also claimed primacy over the bishops of Africa—a claim injurious to the prerogative of Carthage[1]. In Egypt, and the adjoining Libya and Pentapolis, the bishop of Alexandria was, at the time of the Nicene and Antiochene Councils, probably the only metropolitan. In Syria, the metropolitan of Cæsarea (Palæstina) was among the bishops subordinate to the see of Antioch. When we come to Asia Minor and the region known nowadays as the Balkan Peninsula we find three great dioceses, of which express mention is made in the second canon of the Council of Constantinople (A.D. 381). This word 'diocese,' like 'province' and 'metropolis,' came into the vocabulary of the Church from that of the Empire. The three dioceses mentioned in the Constantinopolitan Canon just referred to are (1) Asiana, (2) Pontica, (3) Thracia[2]. In the Asian diocese, the

---

[1] The pretensions of the bishop of Rome, however, encountered sturdy resistance in Africa. See Salmon, *Infallibility of the Church*, pp. 407, 414, 415, Robertson, *History of the Christian Church*, II. pp. 149—151, 236, 237.

[2] Concil. Const. Can. II. τοὺς ὑπὲρ διοίκησιν ἐπισκόπους ταῖς ὑπερορίοις ἐκκλησίαις μὴ ἐπιέναι μηδὲ συγχέειν τὰς ἐκκλησίας, ἀλλὰ κατὰ τοὺς κανόνας τὸν μὲν Ἀλεξανδρείας ἐπίσκοπον τὰ ἐν Αἰγύπτῳ μόνον οἰκονομεῖν, τοὺς δὲ τῆς Ἀνατολῆς ἐπισκόπους τὴν Ἀνατολικὴν μόνην διοικεῖν, φυλαττομένων τῶν ἐν τοῖς κανόσι τοῖς κατὰ Νίκαιαν πρεσβείων τῇ Ἀντιοχέων ἐκκλησίᾳ, καὶ τοὺς τῆς Ἀσιανῆς διοικήσεως ἐπισκόπους τὰ κατὰ τὴν Ἀσιανὴν μόνον διοικεῖν, καὶ τοὺς τῆς Ποντικῆς τὰ τῆς Ποντικῆς μόνα, καὶ τοὺς τῆς Θρᾳκικῆς τὰ τῆς Θρᾳκικῆς μόνον διοικεῖν......τὰ καθ' ἑκάστην ἐπαρχίαν ἡ τῆς ἐπαρχίας σύνοδος διοικήσει, κατὰ τὰ ἐν Νικαίᾳ ὡρισμένα. In the fifth Canon of Nicæa, another phrase

leading see was that of Ephesus, though at the time of the Canon Iconium also, and the Pisidian Antioch, were prominent and important. In the Pontic diocese, the lead was taken by the Cappadocian Cæsarea, and in the Thracian the metropolis was Heracleia. Before the foundation of Constantinople, Thessalonica was the most important city in all the countries between the Danube and Cape Malea, and the Church of Thessalonica, founded by St Paul, and connected with a city of such pre-eminence, was naturally the 'metropolitan' Church of Thrace, Macedonia and Illyricum. But Thessalonica appears already to have been reckoned, along with sees subordinate to it in Macedonia and Illyricum, as belonging to the jurisdiction of Rome—and the same is to be said of Corinth with Achæa (or Greece) and even Crete[1]. These regions remained

of secular origin should be noticed—τὸ κοινὸν τῶν ἐπισκόπων, meaning the episcopate of the province (ἐπαρχία). Compare the phrase Κοινὸν Κυπρίων on coins of Cyprus belonging to the first three centuries of the Christian era, and the use of τὸ κοινὸν in Thucyd. IV. 78; also 'commune Siciliæ' in Cicero, *Verr.* Act. II. Lib. ii. 114 and 145. For the κοινὸν of Asia, the κοινὸν of Bithynia, etc., see Mommsen, *Provinces of the Roman Empire*, I. pp. 344—350.—'Diœcesis' occurs in Cicero, *ad Fam.* III. viii. 4, XIII. lxvii., in the sense of a district within a province. Three 'dioceses' of Asia, he says, were attached to his Cilician province. See Lightfoot, *Colossians*, pp. 7—8 for further illustrations. In *C.I.G.* 4693 Egypt is called a διοίκησις. The use of the word to denote a group of provinces appears to have come in with the reorganization of the Empire by Diocletian. The ecclesiastical 'dioceses' mentioned in Conc. Const. Can. II. appear to have generally coincided in extent with the civil dioceses, Aegyptus, Oriens, Pontica, Asiana, Thracia. For provinces included in these dioceses, see Bury's *Gibbon*, II. 550—552.

[1] In the civil divisions of the Empire, Crete was included in the diocese of Macedonia, after the breaking-up of the diocese of the Mœsias into the two dioceses of Dacia and Macedonia. The Macedonian diocese included Macedonia, Thessaly, Epirus, Achaia (i.e. Greece), and Crete. Jurisdiction

within the ecclesiastical jurisdiction of Rome down to the age of the Iconoclast controversy (A.D. 733)[1]. The predominant position of Constantinople led to the extension of the bishop's authority over the Asian and Pontic dioceses or 'exarchates,' as we learn from the 28th Canon of the Council of Chalcedon. The Constantinopolitan Council (Canon 3) had decreed that the Bishop of Constantinople should 'have the prerogative of honour next after the Bishop of Rome' on the express ground of reason that 'Constantinople is New Rome[2].' At Chalcedon the assembled Fathers re-enacted the ruling of their predecessors, and on the same ground. 'For the Fathers reasonably allowed primacy to the throne of the elder Rome, because it was the imperial city, and for the same reason the 150 most godly bishops,' i.e. the Council of Constantinople in A.D. 381, 'assigned equal honours to the most holy throne of the New Rome, judging soundly that the city honoured with the presence of the Imperial Majesty and the Senate should enjoy the same honours and prerogatives as the elder imperial city of Rome, and be made pre-

---

over 'eastern Illyricum,' i.e. Macedonia, Thessaly, Greece, Epirus, was assumed by Innocent I. in pursuance of a policy initiated by Siricius, at the beginning of the fifth century. The pope constituted the bishop of Thessalonica his vicar for the administration of these regions. In 421, Theodosius II. ordered that Macedonia, etc. should form part of the Constantinopolitan 'diocese,' so that the bishops in those provinces should recognize the prelate of the eastern capital as their chief, but within a year or two, at the request of Honorius, he allowed the Roman jurisdiction to be restored.

[1] Paparregopoulos, Ἱστορία τοῦ Ἑλληνικοῦ Ἔθνους, III. 396, 411.

[2] Concil. Const. Can. III. τὸν μέντοι Κωνσταντινουπόλεως ἐπίσκοπον ἔχειν τὰ πρεσβεῖα τῆς τιμῆς μετὰ τὸν τῆς Ῥώμης ἐπίσκοπον, διὰ τὸ εἶναι αὐτὴν Νέαν Ῥώμην.

eminent in the same manner, in ecclesiastical relations, taking the next place[1].' The Chalcedonian Council further ordained that the metropolitans of the Pontic, Asian and Thracian dioceses or exarchates[2], *but these*

---

[1] Concil. Chal. Can. XXVIII. πανταχοῦ τοῖς τῶν ἁγίων πατέρων ὅροις ἑπόμενοι, καὶ τὸν ἀρτίως ἀναγνωσθέντα κανόνα τῶν ἑκατὸν πεντήκοντα θεοφιλεστάτων ἐπισκόπων τῶν συναχθέντων ἐπὶ τοῦ τῆς εὐσεβοῦς μνήμης μεγάλου Θεοδοσίου τοῦ γενομένου βασιλέως ἐν τῇ βασιλίδι Κωνσταντίνου πόλει Νέᾳ Ῥώμῃ, γνωρίζοντες τὰ αὐτὰ καὶ ἡμεῖς ὁρίζομεν καὶ ψηφιζόμεθα περὶ τῶν πρεσβείων τῆς ἁγιωτάτης ἐκκλησίας τῆς αὐτῆς Κωνσταντίνου πόλεως Νέας Ῥώμης. καὶ γὰρ τῷ θρόνῳ τῆς πρεσβυτέρας Ῥώμης, διὰ τὸ βασιλεύειν τὴν πόλιν ἐκείνην, οἱ πατέρες εἰκότως ἀποδεδώκασι τὰ πρεσβεῖα, καὶ τῷ αὐτῷ σκόπῳ κινούμενοι οἱ ἑκατὸν πεντήκοντα θεοφιλέστατοι ἐπίσκοποι τὰ ἴσα πρεσβεῖα ἀπένειμαν τῷ τῆς Νέας Ῥώμης ἁγιωτάτῳ θρόνῳ, εὐλόγως κρίναντες τὴν βασιλείᾳ καὶ συγκλήτῳ τιμηθεῖσαν πόλιν καὶ τῶν ἴσων ἀπολαύουσαν πρεσβείων τῇ πρεσβυτέρᾳ βασιλίδι Ῥώμῃ, καὶ ἐν τοῖς ἐκκλησιαστικοῖς ὡς ἐκείνην μεγαλύνεσθαι πράγμασι, δευτέραν μετ' ἐκείνην ὑπάρχουσαν. καὶ ὥστε τοὺς τῆς Ποντικῆς καὶ τῆς Ἀσιανῆς καὶ τῆς Θρακικῆς διοικήσεως μητροπολίτας μόνους, ἔτι δὲ καὶ τοὺς ἐν τοῖς βαρβαρικοῖς ἐπισκόπους τῶν προειρημένων διοικήσεων, χειροτονεῖσθαι ὑπὸ τοῦ προειρημένου ἁγιωτάτου θρόνου τῆς κατὰ Κωνσταντινούπολιν ἁγιωτάτης ἐκκλησίας, δηλαδὴ ἑκάστου μητροπολίτου τῶν προειρημένων διοικήσεων, μετὰ τῶν τῆς ἐπαρχίας ἐπισκόπων χειροτονοῦντος τοὺς τῆς ἐπαρχίας ἐπισκόπους, καθὼς τοῖς θείοις κανόσι διηγόρευται. χειροτονεῖσθαι δέ, καθὼς εἴρηται, τοὺς μητροπολίτας τῶν προειρημένων διοικήσεων παρὰ τοῦ Κωνσταντινουπόλεως ἀρχιεπισκόπου, ψηφισμάτων συμφώνων κατὰ τὸ ἔθος γινομένων καὶ ἐπ' αὐτὸν ἀναφερομένων.

[2] Ἔξαρχος τῶν ἱερέων (pontifex maximus) is found in Plutarch, *Numa* 10. On the 34th 'Apostolic' Canon (see above, p. 45, n. 2) the *Pedalion* has a note, pointing out that the first bishop of a 'nation' (ἔθνος) or province is called, in the sixth Canon of the Council of Sardica, 'bishop of the metropolis' and 'exarch of the province'—ἐπίσκοπος τῆς μητροπόλεως, ἔξαρχος τῆς ἐπαρχίας. The same note also refers to the Greek version of the records of the Council of Carthage (A.D. 418), in which the chief bishop of a province is called ὁ πρωτεύων or ὁ ἐπίσκοπος τῆς πρώτης καθέδρας (episcopus primæ cathedræ). 'But in the general usage of the majority of canons he is called the metropolitan (μητροπολίτης).' The ninth and seventeenth Canons of the Council of Chalcedon ruled that any bishop or cleric who had a cause to plead against the metropolitan of his province should go to '*the exarch of the diocese*' *or* 'the throne of the imperial City

only, together with bishops in barbarian lands on the frontier of those dioceses, should receive consecration from the see of Constantinople.

Thus four great groups of ecclesiastical provinces were formed, each presided over and directed by a bishop residing in one of the four greatest cities of the Empire. These four patriarchates, as they came to be called, corresponded in number only to the four great prefectures of the Empire—in boundaries they were

of Constantine.'—In a long note upon the former of these two Canons the *Pedalion* points out that the Patriarchs of Constantinople never claimed universal jurisdiction on the strength of the ruling thus worded, from which it is to be inferred that the fathers assembled at Chalcedon never intended to confer such authority upon the see of New Rome. By the 'exarch of the diocese' is meant, not the metropolitan of the province, for the diocese is a group of provinces, but the metropolitan of the diocese, i.e. the metropolitan who is first among the metropolitans associated in one diocesan group. At the present day, proceeds the author of the note in the *Pedalion* (p. 193), though some metropolitans are called 'exarchs' they have no effective superiority over other metropolitans. The 'exarchs of dioceses' at the time of the Council of Chalcedon, then, occupied a position superior to that of other metropolitans, without being equal to that of patriarchs. According to Zonaras, the metropolitan bishops of Cæsarea (in Cappadocia), Ephesus, Thessalonica, and Corinth were 'exarchs,' distinguished by wearing πολυσταύρια (a sort of chasuble embroidered with crosses) when they officiated in church. The exarchate, however, appears to have ceased to exist, save as a title of honour, soon after the Council of Chalcedon. So far as the evidence of conciliar canons goes, the only exarchs then existing were those of the Pontic, Asian, and Thracian dioceses, which were all included in the patriarchate of Constantinople. The ninth Canon of Chalcedon, therefore, really gave the archbishop of the New Rome appellate jurisdiction over the dioceses just named, the practical consequence being that the exarchic jurisdiction came to an end. No mention, apparently, of exarchs is made in the laws of Justinian relating to clerical litigation. Again, the Council of Chalcedon, in its ninth and seventeenth Canons, had in view only the patriarch of Constantinople and the metropolitans recognized as subject to his primacy.

quite different from them, Rome, for instance, being the headquarters of an ecclesiastical jurisdiction extending over regions included in no less than three out of the four prefectures, while the bishop of Antioch, if not the bishop of Alexandria also, exercised spiritual authority in lands outside the boundaries of the Roman Emperor's dominions[1]. The language of the 20th Canon of Chalcedon, however, proves that the Fathers of Christendom had, as a rule, tended to adapt the territorial organization of the Church to that of the civil state. This appears again in the history of the see of Jerusalem or Ælia Capitolina. Jerusalem was, and is, the mother-city of the Christian religion. The city was destroyed by Titus in A.D. 70, but a town of some sort formed itself after a time on the ruins of the city. It was not in Jerusalem, however, but in Cæsarea, the provincial capital, that Palestinian Christianity had the headquarters of its government, even after the foundation of Ælia Capitolina as a Roman colony. The Christian community in Jerusalem naturally cherished a desire to take precedence of Cæsarea, but this ambition was not satisfied till the fifth century, when Jerusalem was constituted a ‘patriarchal’ see, the bishop of Jerusalem thenceforth having metropolitans under him, and recognizing only a ‘precedence of honour’ in his brethren of Rome, Constantinople, Alexandria and Antioch, the sphere of the new patriarchal jurisdiction consisting of territories hitherto included in that of Antioch, viz. the three regions into which Palestine was then divided. This settlement was arrived at in the Council of Chalcedon, A.D. 451. It was a compromise, for Juvenal, the

---

[1] The jurisdiction of Alexandria extended into Abyssinia.

bishop of Jerusalem, who had been scheming for twenty years past to free himself from subordination to the Antiochene prelate, had claimed the region of Arabia, and part at least of Phœnicia, as his diocese[1].

The title 'patriarch' is not found in the Canons of the first four Œcumenical Synods, but it appears, from the quotations given by M. Gedeon in the preface to his 'Πατριαρχικοὶ πίνακες,' to have been in use before the date of the Council of Constantinople. According to M. Gedeon, it was taken over by the Church from the Old Testament (i.e. the Greek version), II. Chron. xxvi. 12, πᾶς ὁ ἀριθμὸς τῶν πατριαρχῶν τῶν δυνατῶν εἰς πόλεμον δισχίλιοι ἑξακόσιοι—'the whole number of the chief of the fathers of the mighty men of valour was two thousand and six hundred.' M. Gedeon might have added Acts ii. 29, 'the patriarch David,' and vii. 8, 'Jacob begat the twelve patriarchs'; and Hebrews vii. 4, where Abraham is called 'the patriarch.' But the ecclesiastical use of the title resembles not so much the Scriptural as the use established for nearly three centuries in Jewry after the suppression of Bar-Khokba's insurrection and the foundation of Ælia Capitolina on the site of Jerusalem. The Jews dispersed throughout the Roman Empire found a new bond of union in common acknowledgment of the authority of a 'patriarch' who resided in Tiberias. This patriarch appointed subordinate ministers, among them being his envoys to the children of Israel scattered abroad in the lands of the heathen; these envoys were called 'apostles.' 'It is a singular spectacle,' wrote Dean Milman, 'to behold a nation dispersed in every region of the world, without

[1] Robertson, *History of the Christian Church*, II. pp. 227—229.

murmur or repugnance, submitting to the regulations, and taxing themselves to support the greatness, of a supremacy which rested solely on public opinion, and had no temporal power whatever to enforce its decrees.' The Jewish Patriarchate of Tiberias is curiously like the mediæval Papacy, and the resemblance is heightened by the fact that the Jews inhabiting the lands to the east of the Roman Empire observed allegiance to a spiritual sovereign, the 'Prince of the Captivity,' resident in Babylon, who stood over against the Western prelate very much as the Patriarch of Constantinople over against the Pope[1].

The Patriarchate of Tiberias was abolished by an edict of the younger Theodosius, about A.D. 420[2]. By that time the title patriarch had come into accepted use among Christians, though that use was as yet not quite fixed. In the passages quoted or referred to by M. Gedeon, we find it applied by Gregory Nazianzene to his father, the bishop of Nazianzus, by Gregory Nyssene to the bishops assembled at Constantinople in the Second Œcumenical Council, by Theodosius II. to John Chrysostom and Leo of Rome. Leo is also designated 'patriarch' in the 'Acta' of the Council of Chalcedon. A passage of considerable importance in the history of the title is given at length by M. Gedeon, from the eighth chapter of the fifth book of Socrates' *Ecclesiastical History*. The passage runs as follows: 'They,' i.e. the Council of Constantinople, 'established

[1] Milman, *History of the Jews*, ch. xix. Gibbon, *Decline and Fall*, II. 73, 74 (Bury's ed.).

[2] Bingham, *Antiquities*, bk II. ch. xvii. § 4 (vol. I. p. 197. Oxford edition of 1855). Bingham seems to think that the Jewish patriarchate dated from the first century, C.E.

patriarchs, among whom they distributed the provinces, so that diocesan bishops should not interfere with churches outside the limits of their jurisdiction—a matter in which irregularity had set in by reason of the persecutions. Nectarius obtained the capital (Constantinople) and Thrace as his portion. The patriarchate (πατριαρχεία) of the Pontic diocese fell to Helladius, successor of Basil in the bishopric of Cæsarea in Cappadocia, Gregory of Nyssa, Basil's brother, and Otreius, bishop of Melitene in Armenia. The Asian diocese was assigned to Amphilochius of Iconium and Optimus of the Pisidian Antioch, while the affairs of Egypt became the charge of Timothy, bishop of Alexandria. The diocese of the East was given to the same bishops as before—Pelagius of Laodicea and Diodorus of Tarsus—under reservation of the privileges of the Church of Antioch. These were given to Meletius, who was then present[1].'

[1] Socrates *H. E.* v. 8. The 150 bishops assembled at Constantinople in 381 πατριάρχας κατέστησαν διανειμάμενοι τὰς ἐπαρχίας, ὥστε τοὺς ὑπὲρ διοίκησιν ἐπισκόπους ταῖς ὑπερορίοις ἐκκλησίαις μὴ ἐπιβαίνειν, τοῦτο γὰρ πρότερον διὰ τοὺς διωγμοὺς ἐγίνετο ἀδιαφόρως. καὶ κληροῦται Νεκτάριος μὲν τὴν μεγαλόπολιν καὶ τὴν Θρᾴκην· τῆς δὲ Ποντικῆς διοικήσεως Ἑλλάδιος ὁ μετὰ Βασίλειον Καισαρείας τῆς Καππαδοκῶν ἐπίσκοπος, Γρηγόριος ὁ Νύσσης ὁ Βασιλείου ἀδελφός (Καππαδοκίας δὲ καὶ ἥδε πόλις), καὶ Ὀτρήϊος ὁ τῆς ἐν Ἀρμενίᾳ Μελιτηνῆς τὴν πατριαρχίαν ἐκληρώσατο. Τὴν Ἀσιανὴν δὲ λαγχάνουσιν Ἀμφιλόχιος ὁ Ἰκονίου καὶ Ὄπτιμος ὁ Ἀντιοχείας τῆς Πισιδίας. τὸ δὲ κατὰ τὴν Αἴγυπτον Τιμοθέῳ τῷ Ἀλεξανδρείας προσενεμήθη. τῶν δὲ κατὰ τὴν Ἀνατολὴν ἐκκλησιῶν τὴν διοίκησιν τοῖς αὐτῆς (αὐτοῖς?) ἐπισκόποις ἐπέτρεψαν, Πελαγίῳ τε τῷ Λαοδικείας καὶ Διοδώρῳ τῷ Ταρσοῦ, φυλάξαντες τὰ πρεσβεῖα τῇ Ἀντιοχέων ἐκκλησίᾳ, ἅπερ τότε παρόντι Μελετίῳ ἔδοσαν. According to this arrangement, the exarchic powers were given to commissions, of three metropolitans in the Pontic diocese, and two each in the Asian and Oriental. In the Oriental diocese, however, the bishop (patriarch) of Antioch had

The phraseology of the Canons of the first four Œcumenical Councils shows that, even as late as the middle of the fifth century, the usage of ecclesiastical titles was still somewhat fluctuating. Of this we have manifest proofs in the 30th Canon of the Chalcedonian Council. In this document we find it recorded that the *bishops* of Egypt deprecated signing 'the letter of the most pious archbishop Leo,' it being the custom 'in the Egyptian diocese' not to take such a step without the cognizance and authorization of 'the *archbishop*' (sc. of Alexandria). They therefore requested dispensation from subscription 'until the consecration of him who should be *bishop* of the great city of Alexandria. It seemed good to the Council that they should be allowed to wait until the " *archbishop* of the great city of Alexandria" should have been ordained.' In the third Canon, again, of the Council of Constantinople, it is decreed that the *bishop* of Constantinople should have the πρεσβεῖα τῆς τιμῆς after the *bishop* of Rome. Similarly, the first four Councils in their Canons speak of the Antiochene prelate as 'bishop,' though the

---

πρεσβεῖα, the nature of which may be inferred from the sixth of the Nicene Canons (*supra*, n. 2, p. 44). The old Roman province of Syria included Cilicia, which again was subsequently included, along with Syria, in the civil diocese 'Oriens.' In Cilicia the chief city was Tarsus, which nevertheless, just as much as Laodicea, yielded precedence to Antioch. Here we note a close correspondence between the civil and the ecclesiastical arrangements, which John of Antioch, half a century later, would have been glad to see rounded off by the subordination of Cyprus to his see. Cyprus, however, though a province of the diocese 'Oriens,' remained independent in matters ecclesiastical. See Hackett, *Church of Cyprus*, pp. 13—21. It is curious that the bishop of Ephesus was not made one of the exarchs of the diocese Asiana.'

patriarchal title must have already been applied to him as well as to his brethren of Rome and Alexandria. In the Quinisext or Trullan Council, Theophilus of Antioch was saluted as ' patriarch,' while in the second Canon of that Council Dionysius, Peter, Athanasius, Cyril and other prelates of Alexandria are entitled ' archbishop,' an honour bestowed in the same document upon Cyprian of Carthage and Basil of Cæsarea. The only ' patriarch ' mentioned in the Canon by that title is Gennadius of Constantinople.

The distribution of the Churches of Christendom into five main groups, having their respective headquarters in Rome, Constantinople, Alexandria, Antioch and Jerusalem, was an established and recognized fact from the time of the Fourth General Council (Chalcedon) onwards. It also came to be felt that the patriarchal title ought to be reserved for the bishops of the five cities just named. But while the occupants of the four Eastern centres of primacy were thenceforth constantly spoken of as patriarchs, till this became their regular designation, the bishops of Rome seem not to have greatly cared to avail themselves of their privilege in this respect. One reason, if not *the* reason, of this was probably the conception they held of their lawful precedence among all the chief pastors of Christendom—a conception which included much more than the Eastern prelates were willing to allow. Thus the title ' Patriarch of Rome ' was never established in permanent use, like the titles ' Patriarch of Constantinople,' ' Patriarch of Alexandria,' etc., and it is quite in agreement with this fact that we find the Popes, in later ages, claiming not merely titular or honorary precedence, but actual power of jurisdiction, over the Patriarchates[1].

With regard to the title ' Patriarch of Constantinople' it is important to note that it is an abbreviation. The full form is ' Archbishop of the City of Constantine, New Rome, and Œcumenical Patriarch ' (Ἀρχιεπίσκοπος Κωνσταντινουπόλεως, Νέας Ῥώμης, καὶ Οἰκουμενικὸς Πατριάρχης). The first part of the title must obviously be traced back to the very earliest period in the history of ' New Rome,' to a time when the name ' patriarch' had hardly obtained a place in the official and legal vocabulary of the Church. The second part sounds as though it were an assumption of world-wide jurisdiction, and a counterblast to the Papal claim of sovereignty over the Church Catholic. Its actual origin, however, is probably to be found in the estimate not unnaturally formed, by Christians in the eastern regions of the Roman Empire, of the importance and authority of the ' Great Church of Constantinople '—especially after the Empire in the West had crumbled into ruins, and Constantinople was indisputably the head of the οἰκουμένη, the ' orbis terrarum ' of the Roman Empire.

[1] The title of *patriarch* was assumed in the West by the metropolitans of Aquileia, in the latter part of the sixth century, but by no means with the consent of the Pope, or on any authority except their own. Their assumption of the title, in fact, emphasized their renunciation of the papal primacy as nullified by acceptance of the ' Three Capitula' propounded by Justinian to the Council convened at Constantinople in A.D. 553. The schism between Rome and Aquileia was not finally healed till the end of the seventh century. Another western patriarchate, that of Grado (Venice), was subsequently created by the Papacy. Robertson, *History of the Christian Church*, II. p. 306, note g. At the present day, the Pope numbers several *patriarchs* in the host of bishops subordinate to him.

Such an estimate the 'Great Church' of Constantinople would hardly be disposed to call in question.

M. Gedeon observes that Theodosius II., in A.D. 438, spoke of St John Chrysostom as οἰκουμενικὸς διδάσκαλος. The imperial compliment, however, in all probability had reference, not to the extent of St John Chrysostom's episcopal jurisdiction, but to the character of his doctrine, and the general esteem in which it was held. At the time of the Council of Chalcedon, certain opponents of Dioscorus referred to Pope Leo as 'the most holy and blessed œcumenical archbishop and patriarch.' This could only have meant that it was the duty and the right of the bishops of Rome to render assistance to any Christian Church 'by heresies distressed.' The same persuasion will best account for the salutation of John the Cappadocian, archbishop of the New Rome, in 518, in the letters received from certain clergy and monks of Syria, denouncing the wickedness of Severus, who then occupied the See of Antioch, but was a fautor of the Monophysite heresy. At the beginning of the sixth century, Constantinople was indubitably the head and metropolis of the οἰκουμένη, i.e. the dominions of the Roman Emperor, the 'circle of lands' Roman, Christian civilized—in those days the epithets were interchangeable—and by that time the οἰκουμένη was identified to a far greater extent with Eastern or Greek than with Western, Latin, Christendom. Nothing could have been more natural than the appeal for aid from the vexed orthodox clergy and monks of Syria to the archbishop of the imperial city. The defence of the οἰκουμένη in its political aspect—i.e. the Empire—devolved upon the monarch; similarly, the defence of the οἰκουμένη in its

spiritual or religious aspect, the Church, might be regarded as part at least of the 'daily charge[1]' of the chief
pastor in 'the house of the kingdom[2].'

[1] II. Cor. xi. 28, ἡ ἐπισύστασίς μοι ἡ καθ' ἡμέραν, ἡ μέριμνα πασῶν τῶν
ἐκκλησιῶν.

[2] In order to arrive at a proper estimate of the title οἰκουμενικὸς
πατριάρχης, one has to ascertain as nearly as possible what meaning it
was likely to convey at the time when it first came into use. It must be
remembered that its local origin was the Hellenic East, and that those by
whom and among whom it originated had a very different conception of
'the world' from ours. The imperial system occupied their mental outlook
to an extent which is difficult for us to appreciate. Some light is thrown
on the subject by the language of Polybius, who may be taken as a representative of Hellenism in other ages besides his own. In Polybius' view,
the Romans were already masters of the world (ἡ οἰκουμένη) when they had
annihilated the power of Macedon and established their hegemony over
the Hellenic commonwealths and the Hellenized kingdoms occupying the
western part of Asia Minor.

Ἡ οἰκουμένη is a phrase that needs to be interpreted in accordance
with its context. There are passages in which it is intended to mean the
whole world, the whole earth—e.g. Ps. xviii. (xix.) 4, S. Matth. xxiv. 14,
Rev. iii. 10, xii. 9, xvi. 14, S. Luke iv. 5. In other passages it has to be
understood with limitations—e.g. Demosthenes, *De Corona*, 242, Polybius,
iii. 1, vi. 1 and 50, viii. 4, Acts xi. 28, xvii. 6, xix. 27, S. Luke ii. 1.

The patriarchs of Constantinople could hardly have intended to claim
an exclusive right to the use of the title 'œcumenical.' It was a title that
any or all of the four other patriarchs could have assumed. The patriarch
of Alexandria, in fact, was distinguished by the title κριτὴς τῆς οἰκουμένης.
According to one account, the origin of this title was the assumption by
Cyril of Alexandria, at the request of Celestine, of the function of papal
delegate or deputy at the Council of Ephesus in 431. This explanation,
however, can hardly be reconciled with the fact that Celestine sent three
representatives to that Council. Another account connects the title with
the duty assigned by the Council of Nicæa to the bishop of Alexandria
with reference to the observation of Easter. The bishop of Alexandria
was to notify to the bishop of Rome, year by year, the day, as ascertained
by astronomical investigation, on which the next Easter festival was to be
held, and the bishop of Rome was to communicate this information to the
world at large. However that may be, we find no patriarch of Alexandria

Nothing, probably, was heard in Rome in 518 of the high-sounding title bestowed upon John the Cappadocian in the letter from the Syrian clergy and monastics. At any rate, no objections appear to have been made by Pope Hormisdas. Even if any had been made, very little account of them would have been taken by Justinian, who had a high-handed fashion of dealing with papal opposition. In edicts and 'novellæ' Justinian gave a legal character to the title 'œcumenical bishop,' which he bestowed upon John the Cappadocian's successors, Epiphanius, Anthimus, Theunas and Eutychius. It was no innovation, therefore, when the patriarch John the Faster, in A.D. 587, assumed the title, but his action provoked the severe displeasure of his contemporaries in the Roman See, Pelagius II. and Gregory the Great, who declared that such pride and self-exaltation marked a man out as a forerunner of the Antichrist. Jealousy of the pre-eminence of Constantinople can hardly be left out of the account in explaining the attitude taken up by Pelagius and Gregory. But in fairness to Gregory, if not to his predecessor also, it must be pointed out that he understood the title 'œcumenical bishop' to mean 'sole bishop,' implying a claim to be the fountain of episcopal authority for the whole Church, and when Eulogius of Alexandria addressed him in a letter as 'universal Pope,' Gregory refused the title, as enriching him unlawfully at his brother's expense. 'If,' he said, 'you style me universal Pope, you deny that you are *at all* that which you own me to be universally[1].'

setting up a literal claim to 'judge the world' by representing his see as the supreme court of Christendom.

[1] Robertson, *History of the Christian Church*, II. 376—379.

In defence of the Constantinopolitan prelates it is urged that they never thought of claiming to be ' œcumenical ' in the sense ascribed to the word by Pope Gregory. The claim involved in its assumption, however, cannot have been less than a claim to primacy in the Roman Empire, within the pale of which, they might argue, the old imperial metropolis was no longer included, or, if it was included, its rank was that of a provincial town, of less consequence than Ravenna, where the imperial Exarch resided. One cannot help suspecting a covert design to reverse the relations of Rome and Constantinople on the strength of the political situation, and so effecting a development of the principle underlying the third Canon of Constantinople and the twenty-eighth of Chalcedon, in resisting which the Popes had a good deal of right and reason on their side. Gregory's remonstrances and censures, however, were of no avail to the end for which they were uttered, the persuasion of the archbishop of the New Rome to discard the title ' œcumenical.' The persistency of their eastern brethren in this matter may have been an inducement to Leo II. to acquiesce in the ascription of the much-disputed title of honour to him by the Emperor Constantine Pogonatus in A.D. 682, and the compliment was returned a little over a century later, when the papal legate addressed Tarasius as ' œcumenical patriarch ' in the Second Council of Nicæa, A.D. 787[1]. This concession, however, on the part of the Pope can hardly have been made without some counterbalancing reservation, possibly an *a fortiori* argument based on the second Canon of the Council of Constantinople in A.D. 381, which would have run as follows—

[1] *Pedalion*, p. 209 n.

the See of Constantinople is recognized by the Canon as being next in honour and exaltation to the See of Rome; the Patriarch of Constantinople claims the title of οἰκουμενικός; much more, then, may the Pope claim that title.

The explanation given by the Greeks at the present day, as set forth in the *Pedalion*, is the same as the explanation elicited by the criticisms of Anastasius, the Librarian of the Papal See, in the ninth century. 'While I was residing at Constantinople,' says Anastasius, 'I often used to take the Greeks to task over this title, censuring it as a sign of contempt or arrogance. Their reply was that they called the patriarch "œcumenical" (which many render by "universal") not in the sense of his being invested with authority over the whole world, but in virtue of his presiding over a certain region thereof, which is inhabited by Christians. What the Greeks call *œcumene* is not only what the Latins call *orbis*, and from its comprehensiveness, orbis *universalis*, but also answers to "habitatio" or "locus habitabilis."' In like manner the author of the long note on the 28th Canon of Chalcedon in the *Pedalion*, pp. 207—209. 'The word οἰκουμενικὸς means either of two things. First, it may be understood comprehensively in relation to the whole Church, in the sense that the œcumenical bishop is one who possesses peculiar and monarchical authority over the whole Church. Or, secondly, it means a large part of the inhabited earth. Many kings, though not lords over the whole earth, are thus entitled "masters of the world" (so, for instance, Evagrius speaks of Zeno) in so far as they have dominion over a large part of it. In the first significance of the title, the patriarch of Constantinople is never styled "œcumenical," nor is the patriarch of Rome, nor anyone else, save Christ alone, the true Patriarch of all the world, to whom hath been given all power in heaven and upon earth. It is in the second sense that the patriarch of Constantinople is styled "œcumenical" as having subject to his authority a great part of the world, and furthermore as being a zealous defender of the faith and the traditions of the Councils and the Fathers, not only in his own province (διοίκησις), but in the others as well.'

The meaning thus attached to the title is not very closely defined, but this lack of definiteness leaves room for considerable latitude in practical application. It enables a patriarch of Constantinople to intervene in ecclesiastical affairs outside the limits of his ordinary jurisdiction just so far as the occasion allows him to do so safely, without exposing himself to the charge either of stretching himself beyond his measure or of failing to come up to it.

In the course of more than fifteen centuries since the foundation of Constantinople, the territorial limits of the patriarch's jurisdiction have frequently been changed. They were enlarged by Leo the Iconoclast, who withdrew Crete, Greece and Macedonia from the Roman 'diocese' and assigned them to that of Constantinople. From 923 to 972 Bulgaria was a separate patriarchate, in virtue of the treaty made between Romanus I. and Simeon, the king of Bulgaria. The conquest of Bulgaria by John Zimiskes in 972 deprived the Bulgarian primate of his patriarchal dignity and title, but left him 'autocephalous,' i.e. independent of any patriarch. About ten years later the headquarters of the Bulgarian kingdom

were transferred to Achrida in Illyria, and with them the
primatial see, the occupant of which bore the title of
Archbishop of Prima Justiniana, Achrida and All Bulgaria. The measure of independence claimed for the
See of Achrida was no small one, as the coronation of
Theodore Angelos showed, this ceremony being performed by the Bulgarian primate at Thessalonica (A.D.
1222). From the early part of the thirteenth century to
the time of the capture of Constantinople by the Turks
there were two other independent archbishoprics in the
Balkan Peninsula, viz. Pekion in Servia and Tirnova in
Bulgaria. These independent jurisdictions were recognized by the œcumenical patriarchate as useful checks
and restraints upon the archbishopric of Achrida, the
attitude of which was generally one of hostility to the
East-Roman Empire. They were both reincorporated
in the patriarchate after the fall of Constantinople,
though Pekion regained its independence for a time
towards the close of the seventeenth century, only to
surrender it again in 1766. In the following year the
archbishop of Achrida surrendered his autonomy, and
together with the bishops subordinate to him took his
place under the jurisdiction of Constantinople[1].

At one time the patriarch of Constantinople claimed
authority over the Church of Russia, which was first
founded by Greek missionaries in the tenth century.

---

[1] Hackett, *Church of Cyprus*, pp. 250—283. Finlay, *History of Greece*,
II. 311. 'The Arch-Bishop of Epikion in Servia, who hath 16 Bishops
under him, and of Ocrida which hath 18, are not subject to the Patriarch
of Constantinople'—Paul Ricaut, *The present State of the Greek and
Armenian Churches, Anno Christi* 1678. Smith, *Greek Church* (London,
1680), pp. 73, 74.

Towards the close of the sixteenth century, when the Principality of Muscovy had become a large and powerful empire, a new patriarchate was created, having its local habitation in Moscow. The new line of patriarchs, however, did not continue for more than 111 years, the place of the patriarch, as the chief ecclesiastical authority, being taken in the eighteenth century, in the last years of Peter the Great, by the 'Spiritual College,' or, as it was subsequently named, the 'Most Holy Governing Synod,' consisting at first of ten, subsequently of eight members[1].

[1] The Russian patriarchate was first established by the patriarch of Constantinople, Jeremias II., on his own initiative, in January, A.D. 1589. Jeremias was then making a tour in Muscovy, collecting the alms of the orthodox faithful for the support of the œcumenical patriarchate. A curious account of the event, written in decapentesyllabic metre, was drawn up by Arsenios, Metropolitan of Elassona, who accompanied Jeremias II. on his tour. See K. N. Satha's biography of Jeremias II. (Athens, 1870). The last patriarch of Moscow, Adrian, died A.D. 1700. In A.D. 1721 the 'Spiritual College' or 'Most Holy Governing Synod' was instituted. The metropolitans of Kiev, Moscow, and S. Petersburg, and the 'Exarch' of Georgia, are ex-officio members. See *The Russian Church and Russian Dissent*, by A. F. Heard (New York, 1887), pp. 118, 124—5, 156—7.

The Princes of Moscow assumed the title of Tsar in A.D. 1547. Their dominions at that time covered an area of about 500,000 square miles. This had been increased to 1½ million square miles in 1584 (the last year of Ivan the Terrible) by conquests to the east and north, reaching beyond the Urals. In 1584, then, Moscow had become the capital of a very considerable realm, and this appears to have suggested the creation of a patriarchate for the befitting exaltation of the Church in the new Christian empire. At any rate, it was avowedly on the principle expressed in the twenty-eighth Canon of Chalcedon, and the third of Constantinople (A.D. 381), that the synod assembled in Constantinople in A.D. 1593 decreed that 'the throne of the most pious and orthodox city of Moscow should be, and be called, a patriarchate (πατριαρχεῖον).' See K. N. Satha, *op. cit.*, pp. 86 and 88. This synod, however, would not allow the new patriarchate to rank third, as had been originally proposed, but appointed it to the fifth place, in order

At the beginning of the nineteenth century the jurisdiction of the œcumenical patriarch extended over the greater part of the Balkan Peninsula, and on the Asiatic side of the Bosphorus and Hellespont as far as the Taurus range in the one direction and the country round Trebizond in the other. Since that time the boundaries of the patriarch's jurisdiction have been greatly contracted by reason of the political changes which have taken place in South-eastern Europe. In Greece, Roumania, Servia and Bulgaria new states have come into existence, and so many provinces have been withdrawn from the œcumenical patriarchate. On the other hand, the Asiatic provinces remain unchanged. Crete also is still included in the patriarchate[1].

not to innovate upon the ruling of the Quinisext Council in its thirty-sixth Canon. 'The Muscovites and Russians,' wrote Ricaut in 1678, 'have their own Patriarch of late years, yet they acknowledge a particular respect and reverence unto the See of Constantinople, to which they have recourse for counsel and direction in all difficult points controverted in Religion.' Ricaut, *op. cit.*, p. 83.

[1] Not only in the extent and boundaries of the patriarchal jurisdiction, but also in the number and location of metropolitan and episcopal sees included within it, have there been changes. The Ἔκθεσις νέα ᾿Ανδρονίκου βασιλέως, drawn up by or by order of the Emperor Andronicus I., about A.D. 1320, contains the names of 109 metropolitan sees subordinate to the throne of Constantinople. Of the see-cities mentioned in this catalogue, some have ceased to exist, and had even ceased to exist at the time when the catalogue was drawn up. The rest, for the most part, are places of no great importance. Many of the sees, again, are no longer in existence, and no less than twelve are in the kingdom of Greece and therefore no longer subject to the œcumenical throne. It should be remembered that in A.D. 1320 the boundaries of the Eastern Empire, both in Asia and in Europe, had undergone a great deal of shrinking. A catalogue of metropolitan sees existing in the patriarchate about A.D. 1640, drawn up by Philippus Cyprius, would indicate about 40 as the number of such sees at that date. The catalogue, however, is defective. It appears to have

In the East-Roman or 'Byzantine' Empire the patriarch of Constantinople was the 'first subject of the realm.' The exalted nature of his position was shown by the privileges which the court-etiquette conceded to him. He was the only person in the Empire to greet whom the sovereign rose from his seat. At the ἀποκοπτή, the table set apart for the Emperor in a State banquet, the patriarch was the guest most honoured and distinguished. The two most important constituents of the State, according to the theory of the mediæval Empire, were the Emperor and the Patriarch (τῆς πολιτείας τὰ μέγιστα καὶ ἀναγκαιότατα μέρη βασιλεύς ἐστι καὶ πατριάρχης)[1]. But just because the patriarchate was so exalted an office in the Church, and consequently in the State, the personality of its occupant could not be a matter of indifference to the temporal sovereign. To make use of the hierarchy as agents of the imperial power was one of the principles of government in the Roman Empire after it became Christian. Both the vicinity of the patriarchal residence and the imperial palace in Constantinople, and the loss of Egypt, Syria,

been originally drawn up ages before the time of Philippus Cyprius, by whom certain notes were added here and there. In it Calabria and Sicily appear as regions subject to the jurisdiction of Constantinople—a state of affairs past and over long before the seventeenth century. Thomas Smith, in his *Account of the Greek Church* (A.D. 1680), gives a list of 79 sees, metropolitan and diocesan taken together. There are now 74 metropolitan and 20 diocesan sees in the patriarchate. The following bishoprics, after the liberation of Greece, and in consequence of that event, were withdrawn from the patriarchal jurisdiction—viz. 1 Athens, 2 Thebes, 3 Naupactus, 4 Corfu, 5 Patras, 6 Lacedæmon, 7 Argos (Nauplia), 8 Paros and Naxos, 9 Andros, 10 Chalcis (Eubœa), 11 Pharsala, 12 Larissa, 13 Monemvasia. These are all found in the Catalogues given by Philippus Cyprius.

[1] Paparregopoulos, Ἱστορία τοῦ Ἑλληνικοῦ Ἔθνους, IV. pp. 9—12.

and the West in consequence of Saracen, Lombard and Frankish aggressions, stimulated the tendency of the supreme temporal authority to influence and determine elections to the throne of St John Chrysostom. Hence the history of the relations of the two powers, the imperial and the patriarchal, is a record, not perhaps of incessant conflict, but certainly of frequent collisions. The Emperors made no objection to having the forms of election to the patriarchal see by bishops, clergy, and people (the last being represented by the senators) observed with all due dignity, so long as the person of him who obtained election was acceptable to them. Often enough, the election was a mere formality, in which the bishops, clergy and people did not so much ratify, as testify their grateful acceptance of, an imperial nomination. But when the election escaped imperial control, great troubles were certain to arise, and while the Emperor could forcibly depose and imprison a patriarch whom he disliked, the patriarch, or on his behalf the monks, who swarmed in Constantinople, and on whose allegiance the patriarchal power was chiefly based, might by appealing to the people at large call forth turbulent demonstrations of a sort which even a strong ruler would not regard with complete indifference.

The determination of the succession by imperial influence may be said to have been the rule during the millennial existence of the East Roman Empire. After the Turkish Conquest, the patriarch became the chief of the Sultan's Christian subjects, and his position was rather improved than otherwise, for the sovereign, though reserving power to ratify and confirm elections, was disposed to leave those elections in other respects free.

Formal confirmation of election had been exercised by the Christian Emperors, from whose hands the patriarchs received the δεκανίκιον, or jewelled crozier symbolic of governing authority. M. Gedeon refers to Codinus and Phranza for descriptions of the ceremonies of confirmation and investiture[1]. Phranza's account is especially interesting, as it is a record in detail of the manner in which the tradition of the Christian Emperors was perpetuated by the Mohammedan Sultans.

'On the third day after the storming of the city, the Emir held high festival of rejoicing over his victory, and made proclamation that all, both small and great, who had concealed themselves anywhere in the city should come forth, and live in freedom and quietness, also that such as had fled from the city in fear of the siege should return, every man to his own house, and abide, every man in his occupation and religion, even as it had been aforetime. Moreover, he commanded that they should make them a patriarch in accordance with established customs, for the patriarchate was vacant. Then the bishops who chanced to be in the city, and a very few clergy of other orders, and laymen, elected to be patriarch the most learned Georgios Scholarios, who was as yet a layman, and gave him the new name of Gennadios. It was an ancient established custom of the Christian Emperors to present the newly-elected patriarch with a δεκανίκιον (crozier) made of gold and adorned with precious stones and pearls, and a horse selected from the imperial stables, gorgeously harnessed with a saddle and saddle-cloth of royal splendour, white silk and gold being the material of the trappings. The patriarch

---

[1] Gedeon, Πατριαρχικοὶ Πίνακες, p. 27 f.

returned to his residence accompanied by the senate, and hailed with applauding shouts. Then he received consecration from the bishops in accordance with standing law and custom. Now the patriarch-designate used to receive the δεκανίκιον from the hands of the Emperor after the following manner. The Emperor sat on his throne, and the whole senate was present, standing with heads uncovered. The great prototype of the palace pronounced a blessing and then recited a short series of petitions (μικρὰν ἐκτενήν), after which the grand domestic sang the canticle "Where the presence of the king is, etc. etc." Then, from the opposite side of the choir, the lampadarios recited the "Gloria" and "King of heaven, etc." The canticle being ended, the Emperor rose to his feet, holding in his right hand the δεκανίκιον, while the patriarch-designate, coming forward with the metropolitan of Cæsarea on one side of him and the metropolitan of Heraclea on the other, bowed thrice to the assembly, and then, approaching the sovereign, did obeisance in the manner due to the imperial majesty. Then the Emperor, raising the δεκανίκιον a little, said, "The Holy Trinity, which hath bestowed upon me the Empire, promoteth thee to be patriarch of New Rome." Thus the patriarch was invested with authority by the hands of the Emperor, to whom he returned the assurance of his gratitude. Then the choirs sang "Master, long be thy days" thrice, and after that came the dismissal. The patriarch, coming down, with lights fixed in the imperial candelabra preceding him, found his horse standing ready, and mounted.

'The infidel, therefore, being desirous to maintain, as sovereign lord of the city, the tradition of the Christian

princes, summoned the patriarch to sit at meat and confer
with him. When the patriarch arrived, the tyrant received
him with great honour. There was a long conference, in
the course of which the Emir made no end of his promises
to the patriarch. The hour for the patriarch's departure
having come, the Emir, on giving him leave to retire,
presented him with the costly δεκανίκιον, and prayed
him to accept it. He escorted the patriarch down to the
courtyard, despite his remonstrances, assisted him to
mount a horse which he had caused to be made ready,
and gave orders that all the grandees of the palace should
go forth with the patriarch. Thus they accompanied
him to the venerable Church of the Apostles, some going
before and some following him. The Emir, you must
know, had assigned the precincts of the Church of the
Apostles for a residence[1].'

Phranza says that the honours, privileges, and ex-
emptions conferred by Mohammed II. upon Gennadios
were intended merely to serve as inducements to the
Christians to settle in Constantinople, which had become
a desolation. The history of the patriarchs, however,
during the reign of Mohammed II., so far as it is known,
shows that if the patriarchate fell into an evil plight, this
was due not so much to Turkish bad faith as to the
prevalence of 'emulations, wrath, strife, seditions, envy-
ings' among the clergy and people. 'Fortunati nimium,
sua si bona nossent' is the conclusion one comes to
after considering, on the one hand, the ample privileges
bestowed upon the patriarchate by the Turkish con-

[1] Georgii Phranza *Historia*, III. xi. Phranza, it should be noticed, calls
Mohammed II. 'Emir,' not 'Sultan.' The title of 'Sultan' appears not to
have been assumed by the Ottoman sovereigns till the sixteenth century.

queror, and on the other, the restless, unsettled state of the Church of Constantinople both under him and under his successors, down to the present day, a clear token whereof is the great number of patriarchal abdications, very few of which have been purely voluntary.

The depositions were not always effected by arbitrary intervention on the part of the secular power. More than once a patriarch was deposed by a synod of metropolitans, which also passed sentence of exile upon him. The execution of the sentence would, of course, be left to the secular authorities.

No doubt much of the disquiet and disorder in the Church of Constantinople during the seventeenth century was due to Jesuit intrigues. But the efforts of the Jesuits would have been comparatively harmless had they not been assisted by the factious spirit rampant among the Greeks. The worst enemies of the Church's peace were to be found among those who were of her own household. With regard to the Turkish Government, we may be permitted to doubt whether it stood in need of any encouragement to perpetrate acts of oppressive intervention, but one cannot be surprised that Sultans and Vizirs, finding themselves appealed to first by one and then by another Christian faction, should have laid hold of the opportunities gratuitously supplied them. If the Christians showed themselves ready to buy the support of the secular power, it was not incumbent upon the secular power, alien in race and religion, to refuse to do business[1].

[1] 'The oppression which the Greeks lie under from the Turks, though very bad and dismal in itself, becomes more uneasy and troublesome by their own horrid Quarrels and Differences about the choice of a Patriarch:

Phranza speaks of the bestowal of the patriarchal crozier (τὸ δεκανίκιον or δικανίκιον) as performed by Mohammed II. in imitation of his Christian predecessors. The ceremony of confirmation or investiture, as described by Phranza, appears not to have been retained in practice for very long. The escort of honour from the Porte to the patriarchal residence may have been continued, but the ceremony of the crozier appears in a document of the sixteenth century as an ecclesiastical and no longer a political one[1]. Moreover, it very soon became customary for the patriarchs to take presents to the Porte, instead of receiving them there. The first four patriarchs, says

there being often times several Pretenders among the Metropolitans and Bishops, and they too making an interest, by large summs of mony, in the Vizir, or the other Bassa's, to attain their ends. He who by his mony and his friends has prevailed...will endeavour to reimburse himself and lay the burden and debt, which he has contracted, upon the Church, which must pay for all: while the rest, who envy his preferment...unite their interest and strength to get him displaced, by remonstrating against his injustice and ill management of affairs, and put up fresh petitions to the Turks, and bribe lustily to be heard. The Turks, glad of such an opportunity of gain, readily enough admit their Complaint, and put out and put in, as they see occasion.......When I reflect upon these Revolutions and Changes, I am filled at the same time with amazement and pity, and cannot but put up this hearty prayer to Almighty God...that He would be pleased to inspire the Grecian Bishops with sober and peaceable counsels.' Smith, *An Account of the Greek Church*, pp. 80—83. Thomas Smith, B.D., Fellow of Magdalen College, Oxford, was chaplain to the English Embassy at Constantinople in the reign of Charles II. From the chapter in his book, out of which the above-quoted passages are taken, it appears that he left Constantinople to return to England in 1671 or 1672. He mentions the protection given by the Embassy to the deposed patriarch Methodius III. in 1671.

[1] Manuel Malaxos, *Historia Patriarchica*, p. 192 (Niebuhr. Bonn, 1839).

Manuel Malaxos[1], were elected without making any present to the Sultan, but after the appointment of Mark Xylocaravis, a junta of immigrants from Trebizond offered the Sultan a thousand florins to obtain his support of their opposition to the patriarch, whom they purposed to remove in favour of a fellow-countryman of theirs, one Symeon, a monk. According to Malaxos, 'the Sultan laughed, and then pondered a long while, considering the enviousness and stupidity of the Romans, and their ungodly ways.' Then he confirmed an assertion made by them to the effect that Mark had promised a thousand florins for the confirmation of his election, though the patriarch had neither promised nor given a copper. The Sultan, however, saw an opening to the establishment of such payments as a regular custom. He took the money offered by Mark's enemies and bade them go and elect as patriarch whomsoever they would. A charge of simony was then brought against Mark, who was put on his trial before a synod, condemned, deposed and anathematized. Symeon was then elected and consecrated, but before very long was deposed by order of the Sultan. Once again money had been talking. The Sultan's stepmother, who appears to have been a Christian, was desirous to promote a friend of hers, the metropolitan of Philippopolis, to honour, and at the same time put an end to the scandalous agitations of the Church caused by the strife between the factions of

---

[1] Malaxos, *op. cit.*, p. 102. τοῦτοι οἱ ἄνωθεν τέσσαροι πατριάρχαι, ὁ Σχολάριος, ὁ Ἰσίδωρος, ὁ Ἰωάσαφ, καὶ ὁ Ξυλοκαράβης, ἔγιναν χωρὶς νὰ δώσουν τοῦ σουλτάνου κανένα δῶρον· μόνον ἔγιναν, καθὼς καὶ ες τὸν καιρὸν τῆς βασιλείας τῶν Ῥωμαίων, ὁποῦ ἐχάριζεν ὁ βασιλεὺς τοῦ πατριάρχου χαρίσματα. Malaxos is one of the chief authorities for the history of the patriarchate in the period A.D 1450—1580.

Symeon and Mark. She therefore brought the Sultan
two thousand florins in a silver dish and told him that
there was a monk who was her friend, and that she
wanted to have him made patriarch. The result of the
proposal was an imperial order for the deposition of
Symeon, who retired to a monastery. Mark was voted
by the synod assembled in the capital, to which he had
appealed for revision of his sentence, to the archbishopric
of Achrida. Dionysius, the protégé of the Sultan's
stepmother, occupied the throne for eight years, and
then, in disgust at a false charge of apostasy, though he
clearly refuted it, abdicated and retired to a monastery
near Cavalla in Macedonia. The synod, in whose
presence he had refuted the charge of apostasy, recalled
Symeon. It was necessary, however, to make sure of
the Sultan's approval, and to this end a deputation
presented itself at the Sublime Porte, bringing a thousand
florins, and so carrying out in act the charge laid in
word against Mark Xylocaravis. But the Defterdar
rejected their petition and the proffered douceur. There
was an entry in the imperial accounts, he said, showing
that the proper amount of the fee was two thousand
florins. This, of course, referred to the transaction
between the Sultan and his stepmother. Of this
matter the members of the synod possibly had no
knowledge at the time, but whether they had or not
made no difference. There was nothing for it but to
sponge up another thousand florins, 'which being done,
says Malaxos, 'the Defterdar ceased from troubling[1].'

Thus an evil precedent was set, and henceforth every
patriarch was expected to pay a fee for the imperial

---

[1] Malaxos, p. 112. καὶ ἔτζη εἰρήνευσεν ὁ τευτερτέρης.

confirmation of his election. To this burden another
was added by the reckless ambition of a Servian monk,
Raphael by name, who procured the final dethronement
of Symeon by the conversion of the investiture fee of
2000 florins into an annual 'kharaj' or tribute, the amount
of the investiture-fee being now fixed at 500 florins[1]. It
was not to be expected, however, that these amounts
should never be exceeded. By the time of Jeremias II.'s
first election to the patriarchate, viz. A.D. 1572, the
investiture fee (πεσκέσιον as Malaxos calls it) was 2000
florins, while the annual 'kharaj' had risen to 4100. In
A.D. 1672, as we learn from Paul Ricaut, the English
Consul at Smyrna, the debts of the patriarchate amounted
to 350,000 piastres, equal to more than £40,000 at the
present day; 'the interest of which increasing daily,
and rigorously extorted by the Power of the most
covetous and considerable Turkish officers, who lend or
supply the Money, is the reason and occasion that the
Patriarch so often summons all his Archbishops and
Bishops to appear at Constantinople, that so they may

---

[1] Malaxos, 1. c. Ἔκαμε δὲ ὁ αὐτὸς πατριάρχης [δηλ. ὁ Συμεών] εἰς τὸν
θρόνον χρόνους τρεῖς, καὶ ἐπέρνα εἰρηνικῶς...ἀμὴ φθονήσας τοῦτο ὁ τῶν σκανδάλων
ἀρχηγὸς καὶ ἐχθρὸς ἡμῶν τῶν Χριστιανῶν, ὁ διάβολος, καὶ ἐφάνη εἰς τὴν μέσιν
ἕνας ἱερομόναχος, ὀνόματι Ῥαφαήλ, τοῦ ὁποίου ἦτον ἡ πατρίδα του ἀπὸ τὴν
Σερβίαν, καὶ εἶχε μεγάλην φιλίαν καὶ παρρησίαν εἰς τὴν πόρτα τοῦ σουλτάνου,
ἔσοντας ὁποῦ ἀγάπουν αὐτὸν οἱ πασιάδες. καὶ...ὑπῆγε καὶ ἐπροσκύνησιν
αὐτούς, καὶ...ἐσυμφώνησε καὶ ἔστερξεν ὅτι νὰ δίδει τὸν καθὲν χρόνον εἰς τὴν
πόρτα τοῦ σουλτάνου χαράτζιον φλωρία χιλιάδας δύο. καὶ τὸ πεσκέσιον
ἔκαμαν νὰ δίδεται ὁπόταν γίνεται νέος πατριάρχης. ἀκούσαντες δὲ τοῦτο οἱ
πασιάδες ἐδέχθησαν τὸν Ῥαφαὴλ τὸν φίλον αὐτῶν ἀσπασίως, καὶ ἀναφορὰν
ἤγουν ἀρτζῆ περὶ τούτου τῷ σουλτάνῳ ἔκαμαν. καὶ ἀκούσας τοῦτο ἐχάρη πολλά,
καὶ ἐν τῷ ἅμα ἔδωκεν ὁρισμόν, καὶ εὔγαλαν τὸν αὐτὸν κύριν Συμεὼν ἀπὸ τοῦ
πατριαρχικοῦ θρόνου. See also the *Historia Patriarchia*, pp. 156, 157,
170, 176, 177, and 193; *Historia Politica*, p. 43, in the same volume of the
Corpus Scriptorum Historiæ Byzantinæ, Bonn, 1849.

consult and agree on an expedient to ease in some measure the present Burden and Pressure of their Debts; the payment of which is often the occasion of new Demands: For the Turks, finding this Fountain the fresher, and more plentifully flowing for being drained, continually suck from this Stream, which is to them more sweet, for being the Blood of the Poor, and the life of Christians[1].' It was, after all, not so much on the dignitaries and authorities of the Orthodox Church, as upon the parish priests and the poor among the people generally, that the fiscal burdens pressed most heavily. The most helpless had to suffer most. What help, indeed, could they expect when their chief shepherds became robbers?

With ironical respect the Orthodox laity, under the Turkish *régime*, spoke of their bishops as '$\delta\epsilon\sigma\pi\sigma\tau\acute{a}\delta\epsilon\varsigma$'—despots. The powers enjoyed by the episcopal order, whose members were made use of by the temporal power as agents of police, were so considerable as to make even an ordinary bishopric an appointment to be coveted—still more a metropolitan see, and most of all the patriarchate[2]. Even apart from the financial opportunities, in the use of which a patriarch or metropolitan could rely on secular assistance, the dignity and honour of 'chief seats in the synagogue' must always have had

[1] Ricaut, *op. cit.* 97—99.

[2] 'The patriarch and the bishops purchased their dignities, and repaid themselves by selling ecclesiastical rank and privileges; the priests purchased holy orders, and sold licenses to marry. The laity paid for marriages, divorces, baptisms, pardons, and dispensations of many kinds to their bishops. The extent to which patriarchs and bishops interfered in family disputes and questions of property is proved by contemporary documents.'— Finlay, *History of Greece*, v. p. 156, cf. p. 150.

considerable attraction for the Greeks, who, even after the Turkish Conquest, esteemed themselves the first of nations[1]. Add to these conditions and circumstances the spirit of jealousy which has been, and still is, the bane of the race—the spirit which gives a Greek army so many generals and so few soldiers[2]—and it is not hard to understand why changes in the occupancy of the patriarchate of Constantinople have been so numerous and frequent[3].

Finlay compares the part played by the Sultans in patriarchal elections with that of the sovereigns of England in appointments to the archbishopric of Canterbury. This comparison, however, is not quite accurate. As a rule, the Sultans have not nominated the successive occupants of the patriarchal throne. Under the Ottoman sovereigns, elections have, if anything, been more free than under their Christian predecessors. But the Padishah must have a list of 'papabili' sent to him, whenever a vacancy occurs in the patriarchate, and he influences the election by notifying to the synod of the 'Great Church' the names of those whom he does *not* wish to see elected. In any case, it is in his power to nullify an election by refusing the necessary 'berat' to the patriarch-designate. The delivery of this document is the formality by which the Sultan confirms the election, invests the person elected with the temporalities of the patriarchal see, and licenses

[1] Finlay, *op. cit.*, v. p. 122.

[2] Ἀμείβετο Γέλων τοῖσδε· 'Ξεῖνε Ἀθηναῖε, ὑμεῖς οἴκατε τοὺς μὲν ἄρχοντας ἔχειν, τοὺς δὲ ἀρξομένους οὐκ ἕξειν.' Hdt. VII. 162. The Athenians, however, showed a better spirit at Platæa—see Hdt. IX. 27 *ad fin.*

[3] Finlay finds that 'mutual distrust was a feature in the character of the higher clergy at Constantinople,' *op. cit.* v. 149.

him to exercise his spiritual authority. Above and beyond all this, the autocratic nature of the Sultan's sovereignty enables him to force a resignation or synodical dethronement whenever he thinks fit. Under an absolute despotism like the Sultanate, the ultimate ground of the patriarch's tenure of office must necessarily be the sovereign's pleasure.

The principle was clearly laid down by the Council of Antioch in the fourth century that in every province the metropolitan and his comprovincials must work in concert and by mutual counsel. In the same way, it is a recognized principle of Church government in Orthodoxy that the patriarch should work in concert with his metropolitans. The records of the patriarchate contain evidence enough and to spare that this principle has been, under the Turkish *régime* at any rate, constantly observed. In the latter part of the nineteenth century its observation was brought under the rule that there should always be twelve metropolitans present in the capital to form the 'perpetual' or 'standing administrative council[1].' These twelve metropolitans are

---

[1] A similar arrangement appears to have been in existence in the seventeenth century. 'The patriarch, in the determination of causes brought before him, has the assistance of twelve of the chief Officers belonging to the Patriarchal Church and dignity. These also assist the Archbishop of Heraclea in vesting and crowning him at his Inauguration, and still retain the same high titles as they did before the Turks came among them. These are as it were his standing Council, to whom he refers the great affairs and concerns of religion.' Thomas Smith, *Greek Church*, p. 78. The officials of the patriarchate, however, would be priests, not bishops. A long list of them is given in the 'Euchologion,' pp. 686 f. (Venice, 1891), together with a description of their several functions. More than one of these titles, by its very form, shows that the patriarchate must have paid the imperial court the sincere compliment

not always the same, for six retire every year, having held office as members of the synod or council for two years, and their places are taken by six others. Each of the metropolitans subordinate to the œcumenical throne takes his place on the synod in his turn, according to seniority. It is not, therefore, the patriarch alone, but rather the patriarch in synod, by whom the chief authority in matters ecclesiastical is exercised in the provinces of the Constantinopolitan Church.

This perpetual administrative synod of the patriarchate must be distinguished from the synod which elects the patriarch[1]. The latter consists of lay representatives

of imitation. There can be no doubt as to the origin of such titles as πρωτονοτάριος, καστρήνσιος, ρεφενδάριος, λογοθέτης, δομέστικος, δεπουτάτος, κουβούκλης.

[1] M. Gedeon, in the preface to his Πατριαρχικοὶ Πίνακες, gives an outline of the history of procedure in elections to the patriarchal throne. Nestorius I., successor of Gregory Nazianzen (A.D. 381), and Proclus (A.D. 434), were examples in an early period of succession by virtue of the Emperor's nomination. Chrysostom's election is described by Socrates, *H. E.* VI. 2. Ψηφίσματι κοινῷ ὁμοῦ πάντων, κλήρου τε φημὶ καὶ λαοῦ, ὁ βασιλεὺς αὐτὸν ᾿Αρκάδιος μεταπέμπεται. διὰ δὲ τὸ ἀξιόπιστον τῆς χειροτονίας παρῆσαν ἐκ βασιλικοῦ προστάγματος πολλοί τε καὶ ἄλλοι ἐπίσκοποι, καὶ δὴ καὶ ὁ τῆς ᾿Αλεξανδρείας Θεόφιλος, ὅστις σπουδὴν ἐτίθετο διασύραι μὲν τὴν ᾿Ιωάννου δόξαν, ᾿Ισίδωρον δὲ ὑπ᾿ αὐτῷ πρεσβύτερον πρὸς τὴν ἐπισκοπὴν προχειρίσασθαι...οἱ μέντοι κατὰ τὰ βασίλεια τὸν ᾿Ιωάννην προέκριναν. ᾿Επειδὴ δὲ κατηγορίας κατὰ Θεοφίλου πολλοὶ ἀνεκίνουν...ὁ προεστὼς τοῦ βασιλικοῦ κοιτῶνος Εὐτρόπιος λαβὼν τὰς ἐγγράφους κατηγορίας ἐπέδειξε τῷ Θεοφίλῳ, εἰπὼν ἐπιλογὴν ἔχειν ἢ χειροτονεῖν ᾿Ιωάννην ἢ τὰς κατ᾿ αὐτοῦ κατηγορίας εἰς ἔλεγχον ἄγεσθαι. Ταῦτα φοβηθεὶς ὁ Θεόφιλος τὸν ᾿Ιωάννην ἐχειροτόνησε. Chrysostom was accordingly consecrated on the 23rd of February, A.D. 398. Germanus was translated from Cyzicus in A.D. 715 ψήφῳ καὶ δοκιμασίᾳ τῶν θεοσεβεστάτων πρεσβυτέρων καὶ διακόνων καὶ παντὸς τοῦ εὐαγοῦς κλήρου καὶ τῆς ἱερᾶς συγκλήτου (Gedeon, p. 16, referring to Scarlati Vizandio, *Constantinopolis*). Leo the Iconoclast seems to have accepted this election without any difficulty, though he found a

as well as of clergy, thus maintaining the old tradition of election by the clergy and people of Constantinople— a tradition which has probably been better observed since the Turkish Conquest than it was previously. In theory, the designation of the patriarch by the votes of

vigorous opponent in Germanus, who, however, resigned in A.D. 730. Anastasius (730—754), Constantine II. (754—766) and Nicetas (766—780), all of them εἰκονομάχοι, were court-nominees. Nicephorus I. (A.D. 806—815), according to Theophanes was elected ψήφῳ παντὸς τοῦ λαοῦ καὶ τῶν ἱερέων, πρὸς δὲ καὶ βασιλέων. The imperial will determined the alternations in Photius' patriarchal career (857—867 and 878—886). M. Gedeon says that κατὰ Φεβρουάριον τοῦ 1059 ὁ αὐτοκράτωρ Ἰσαάκιος ὁ Κομνηνός, ψήφῳ τῶν ἀρχιερέων καὶ τοῦ λαοῦ, ἀνέδειξεν οἰκουμενικὸν πατριάρχην τὸν εὐνοῦχον καὶ μοναχὸν Κωνσταντῖνον Λευχούδην, ἄλλοτε πρωτοβεστιάριον καὶ πρόεδρον τῆς συγκλήτου. In November, 1058, Isaac Comnenus had deposed the famous Michael Cerularius. John VIII. (Xiphilinos) was 'called by the Emperor Constantine Ducas to succeed Constantine III.' in 1064, καὶ πάντες ἐπευφήμισαν εἰς τὴν ψῆφον. Germanus II. (1222—1240) is described as προβληθεὶς πατριάρχης ὑπὸ τοῦ αὐτοκράτορος Ἰωάννου Δούκα τοῦ Βατάτζη. On the death of Callistus II. in 1397, Matthew I. ψήφῳ τῆς συνόδου καὶ προβλήσει τοῦ αὐτοκράτορος ἐκλέγεται διάδοχος. See Gedeon, Πατρ. Πιν., pp. 14—16, 255, 259, 262, 263, 268, 282, 290, 322, 327, 328—9, 384, 458. In the *Historia Patriarchica*, pp. 104—107, and the *Historia Politica*, pp. 39—41, we have instances of the Turkish sovereign putting down one and setting up another patriarch, using the bishops and clergy as his instruments. Theoleptos, about A.D. 1514, got himself forced upon the patriarchate by an imperial berat. In 1741, Sultan Mahmud I. issued a firman regulating procedure in patriarchal elections. One requirement was, that testimony to the character of the person elected should be given by the metropolitans of Heraclea, Cyzicus, Nicomedia, Nicæa, and Chalcedon (the 'γέροντες' as they came to be commonly called), otherwise the election would be treated as invalid. M. Gedeon refers in this connection to Sozomen, *Hist. Eccl.* III. 3, where it is recorded that the Arians objected to the appointment of Paul the Confessor (circ. A.D. 340) on the ground that it had taken place παρὰ γνώμην Εὐσεβίου τοῦ Νικομηδείας ἐπισκόπου καὶ Θεοδώρου τοῦ τῆς ἐν Θράκῃ Ἡρακλείας, οἷς ὡς γείτοσιν ἡ χειροτονία διέφερε. —Another imperial firman, issued by Mustapha II. in 1759, required the announcement of elections by means of a sealed report from the electors.— This method of announcing elections is still followed. The firman also

an assembly representing the whole Christian population of Constantinople, Roumelia and Asia Minor is admirable[1]. In practice, it has been execrable, simply because of the unlimited licence given to ambition and covetousness. Yet even without the disturbing influence of Mohammedan sovereignty these corrupt passions make themselves felt with destructive effect, as witness the events of the last few years in Cyprus, where party strife has kept the archiepiscopal throne vacant from the summer of 1900 to 1909.

Monastics alone are eligible to the episcopate in the Orthodox Church, and the patriarchal residence in Constantinople may be regarded as a monastery, of which the patriarch is the abbot. Since the beginning of the seventeenth century the Church of St George, in the Fanar quarter on the Golden Horn, has been the patriarch's cathedral. This Church occupies the site of the monastery known as the Petrion or Paulopetrion, which was in existence in the reign of Irene in the

required that every patriarch should pay the expenses of his election, which in the eighteenth century were known to run up on occasion to as much as 50,000 piastres (£6,000). Until 1860 ex-metropolitans and ex-bishops, as well as metropolitans and bishops ἐν ἐνεργείᾳ, used to take part in elections, but since that date the representatives of the episcopal order are all metropolitans. There are now four stages in the process of election; (1) voting by a 'convention' of the metropolitans residing in the capital for the time being, of lay representatives, and plenipotentiaries representing twenty-six of the metropolitical sees; (2) submission of the list of 'papabili' to the Porte; (3) election of *three* from the list as emended by the secular authorities; (4) election of the successor from these three, by the metropolitans present.

[1] The lay electors especially represent Constantinople. The metropolitans who take part, either on the spot, or by sending sealed votes, represent the provinces. M. Gedeon observes that the electors must be native subjects of the Sultan.

eighth century, and was for many years the retreat of
the Empress Theodora in the eleventh. It is not a
large building, and externally has no beauty to
recommend it. Within, the chief and almost the only
adornments of any merit are the iconostasion and the
pulpit, works of art which Mr Hutton, one of the most
recent historians of Constantinople, assigns to the
seventeenth century[1]. Most of the buildings of the
'patriarcheion' stand to the west of the church, on
ground which rises somewhat steeply—a circumstance
which enables the group to make somewhat more of
a display than might otherwise have been the case.
There is no magnificence, however, about the residence
of the most notable ecclesiastic in all Orthodox Christendom—nothing to parallel St Peter's and the Vatican.
The difference between the housing of the chief pastors
of the Old and the New Rome, the 'servus servorum
Dei' and the '$οἰκουμενικὸς πατριάρχης$,' is fairly measured
by the apparent difference in character between their
titles.

Originally, the patriarchal residence was in the
neighbourhood of Santa Sophia. After the conquest of
the city, Mohammed II. assigned the Church of the
Holy Apostles, the burial place of Theodora the wife
of Justinian, to Gennadios, but the patriarch, finding
the neighbourhood but scantily inhabited by Christians,
obtained leave to move his residence to the Church of
the Pammakaristos (a special title of the Virgin Mary),
which was the cathedral church of the patriarchate for
130 years, viz. A.D. 1456—1586. The Church of the

---

[1] *Constantinople* in the series of 'Mediæval Towns' (London: J. M.
Dent); by the Rev. W. H. Hutton, B.D.

Apostles was demolished to make room for the mosque which by its name preserves the memory of Mohammed the Conqueror of Constantinople. In 1586 the Sultan took possession of the Pammakaristos Church and turned it into a mosque. The patriarchal cathedra was then placed for a short time in the church of the ‘Panagia of Consolation’ or ‘Healing’ (Παναγία τῆς Παραμυθίας or Θεραπείας), after which it was removed to the Church of St Demetrius in Xyloporta, and thence, in 1601, to its present place[1]. A few icons, books and relics were brought away from the Pammakaristos, and finally deposited in the Church of St George. ‘That which they most esteem,’ wrote Thomas Smith, chaplain to the Embassy, about 1670, ‘is a piece of black Marble; as they pretend, part of that Pillar which formerly stood in the *Prætorium* or Hall of *Pontius Pilate*, to which our Blessed Saviour was tied, when he was whipped; about two foot long, and three or four inches over,... inclosed in brass lattice Grates, that it may not receive prejudice either from devout or sacrilegious persons. For they have a strong imagination, that the dust raised from it, and put into wine, or any way conveyed into the stomach, cures Agues and Fevers almost infallibly. In a brass plate under it I found these six Verses engraven, alluding to the tradition I just now mentioned, which they believe as undoubtedly as if it were Gospell.

> Νῶτον δέδωκας εἰς μάστιγας, Παντάρχα,
> Καὶ πρόσωπον εἰς ῥαπισμάτων ὕβριν.
> Σὴν μαστίγωσιν προσφέρω σοι, οἰκτίρμον,

---

[1] Hutton, *Constantinople*, p. 155. K. N. Satha, Σχεδίασμα περὶ Ἱερεμίου τοῦ Β', σελ. οθ'—πβ'.

Ἰν' ἵλεώς μοι εἴη λατρεύοντί σοι,
Καὶ μάστιγάς σου ἐξ ἐμοῦ ἀποστήσῃς.
Παναγιώτης Νικόσιος εὔχεται.—[1]

In this Church of St George the patriarchs of Constantinople have been formally enthroned for the last
three centuries. As the patriarchs are now, and have
been for a long time past, taken from the metropolitan
episcopate, there is no need of χειροτονία or consecration
properly so called.   In case of one not already consecrated to the episcopate being elected patriarch, the
chief consecrator would be the metropolitan of Heraclea
(Erekli on the Sea of Marmora), the origin of whose
prerogative lies in the fact that Byzantium, at the time
when selected by Constantine to be made the new
imperial capital, was included in the district of which
Heraclea was the chief town[2].   Even when there is no
need of χειροτονία, it is the peculiar function of the
metropolitan of Heraclea to place in the hands of the
patriarch-designate the δεκανίκιον, δικανίκιον or πατε-
ρίτσα, as the patriarchal crozier, a staff terminating in
two serpents' heads, is variously termed.   This symbol
of archipœmenical authority is not indeed the peculiar
badge of the patriarch's dignity.   Serpent-headed croziers

[1] Thomas Smith, *Greek Church*, pp. 60—61.

[2] Gedeon, p. 49. On p. 282, however, in a note, M. Gedeon points
out that there have been occasions when the consecration has been performed by another prelate.   Photius, for instance, had Gregory of Syracuse
for his chief consecrator.   Photius was a layman at the time of his election,
as were also Nectarius (A.D. 381), Paul III. (A.D. 686), Tarasius (A.D. 784),
Nicephorus I. (A.D. 806), Sisinnius II. (A.D. 995) and perhaps John XIII.
(A.D. 1315).   It was not until after the death of Mohammed II. in 1481
that the practice of translation from a metropolitan see became regularly
established.   In the course of eleven centuries, under the Christian
Emperors, there were not so many as twenty instances of translation.

are carried by the Orthodox episcopate generally, with one notable exception, viz. the Archbishop of Cyprus, whose pastoral staff terminates in a globe. The serpents' heads on the pateritsa remind one of the caduceus of Mercury, and the possibility of a connection between the pateritsa and the caduceus is strongly suggested by the fable preserved in the *Astronomia* of Hyginus. According to this story, Mercury once found two snakes fighting, and separated them with his wand. Thenceforth his wand or staff, encircled or twined about by two snakes, became an emblem of peace[1]. This fable is no doubt only a piece of 'ætiology' designed to account for the fact that the snake-entwined staff was a peaceful emblem. Christian bishops, claiming to stand in the apostolical succession, would have the right to style themselves ambassadors of Christ and messengers of peace[2], and their custom of carrying a serpent-headed staff may have originated from some pictorial representation of Christ, or the Apostles, carrying the caduceus as the emblem of reconciliation between God and mankind.

H. T. F. DUCKWORTH.

---

[1] *Dict. of Greek and Roman Antiquities* (Smith's, second edition), art. Caduceus.

[2] II. Cor. v. 20. ὑπὲρ Χριστοῦ οὖν πρεσβεύομεν, ὡς τοῦ Θεοῦ παρακαλοῦντος δι' ἡμῶν· δεόμεθα ὑπὲρ Χριστοῦ, καταλλάγητε τῷ Θεῷ.

THE PATRIARCHS OF CONSTANTINOPLE

In the first column is given the name of the Patriarch: in the second the date of his Patriarchate: the third shows the page on which his life is narrated in M. I. Gedeon's Πατριαρχικοὶ Πίνακες, royal 8vo, Constantinople, 1890, and the fourth how his official life closed.

Acacios	471—489	198	
Agathangelos	1826—1830	688	deposed
Alexandros	325—340	108	
Alexios	1025—1043	317	
Alypios	166—169	94	
Anastasios	730—754	259	
Anatolios	449—458	188	
Andreas, ap.		82	
Anthimos I	536	223	deposed
Anthimos II	1623	552	resigned
Anthimos III	1822—1824	686	deposed
Anthimos IV	1840, 41	694	deposed
Anthimos IV²	1848—1852	698	deposed
Anthimos V	1841, 42	694	
Anthimos VI	1845—1848	697	deposed
Anthimos VI²	1853—1855	699	
Anthimos VI³	1871—1873	705	resigned
Antonios I	821—832	273	
Antonios II	893—895	294	
Antonios III	974—980	310	resigned
Antonios IV	1389, 90	448	deposed
Antonios IV²	1391—1397	449	
Arsacios	404, 05	161	
Arsenios	1255—1260	389	resigned
Arsenios²	1261—1267	392	deposed
Athanasios I	1289—1293	402	resigned
Athanasios I²	1303—1311	405	resigned
Athanasios II	1450	467	resigned
Athanasios III	1634	559	deposed
Athanasios III²	1652	580	resigned
Athanasios IV	1679	602	deposed
Athanasios V	1709—1711	619	deposed
Athenodoros	144—148	92	
Atticos	406—425	164	

Basileios I	970—974	309	deposed
Basileios II	1183—1187	371	deposed
Callinicos I	693—705	253	blinded
Callinicos II	1688	607	deposed
Callinicos II[2]	1689—1693	609	deposed
Callinicos II[3]	1694—1702	611	
Callinicos III	1726	627	
Callinicos IV	1757	648	deposed
Callinicos V	1801—1806	679	deposed
Callinicos V[2]	1808, 09	681	
Callistos I	1350—1354	426	deposed
Callistos I[2]	1355—1363	429	
Callistos II	1397	456	
Castinos	230—237	97	
Chariton	1177, 78	369	
Chrysanthos	1824—1826	687	deposed
Clemes	1667	592	deposed
Constantinos I	674—676	248	
Constantinos II	754—766	262	blinded and beheaded
Constantinos III	1059—1063	327	
Constantinos IV	1154—1156	359	
Constantios I	1830—1834	689	resigned
Constantios II	1834, 35	692	deposed
Cosmas I	1075—1081	333	resigned
Cosmas II	1146, 47	353	deposed
Cosmas III	1714—1716	621	resigned
Cyprianos I	1708, 09	617	resigned
Cyprianos I[2]	1713, 14	621	resigned
Cyriacos I	214—230	96	
Cyriacos II	595—606	236	
Cyrillos I	1612	547	resigned
Cyrillos I[2]	1621—1623	550	deposed
Cyrillos I[3]	1623—1630	553	deposed
Cyrillos I[4]	1630—1634	556	deposed
Cyrillos I[5]	1634, 35	560	deposed
Cyrillos I[6]	1637, 38	562	drowned
Cyrillos II	1632	558	deposed
Cyrillos II[2]	1635, 36	560	deposed
Cyrillos II[3]	1638, 39	567	deposed
Cyrillos III	1652	579	deposed
Cyrillos III[2]	1654	582	deposed
Cyrillos IV	1711—1713	620	deposed
Cyrillos V	1748—1751	641	deposed
Cyrillos V[2]	1752—1757	644	deposed
Cyrillos VI	1813—1818	683	resigned and killed
Cyrillos VII	1855—1860	699	deposed
Cyros	705—711	254	deposed

Demophilos	369—379	126	deposed
Diogenes	114—129	91	
Dionysios I	1467—1472	482	deposed
Dionysios II	1537	504	deposed
Dionysios II[2]	1543—1555	507	
Dionysios III	1662—1665	588	deposed
Dionysios IV	1671—1673	595	deposed
Dionysios IV[2]	1676—1679	599	deposed
Dionysios IV[3]	1683, 84	604	deposed
Dionysios IV[4]	1686, 87	605	deposed
Dionysios IV[5]	1693	610	deposed
Dometios	272—303	98	
Dositheos	1191, 92	375	deposed
Eleutherios	129—136	91	
Epiphanios	520—536	220	
Esaias	1323—1334	417	
Euagrios	369, 70	127	deposed
Eudoxios	360—369	122	
Eugenios I	237—242	97	
Eugenios II	1821, 22	686	
Euphemios	490—496	206	deposed
Eusebios	341, 342	114	Arian
Eustathios	1019—1025	317	
Eustratios	1081—1084	335	deposed
Euthymios I	906—911	296	deposed
Euthymios II	1410—1416	463	
Eutychios	552—565	227	deposed
Eutychios[2]	577—582	231	
Euzoios	148—154	93	
Felix	136—141	91	
Flavianos	447—449	185	killed
Gabriel I	1596	537	
Gabriel II	1657	586	deposed
Gabriel III	1702—1707	614	
Gabriel IV	1780—1785	666	
Gennadios I	458—471	194	
Gennadios II	1454—1456	471	resigned
Georgios I	678—683	250	deposed
Georgios II	1192—1199	376	
Gerasimos I	1320, 21	417	
Gerasimos II	1673—1675	597	deposed
Gerasimos III	1794—1797	673	resigned
Germanos I	715—730	255	resigned
Germanos II	1222—1240	383	
Germanos III	1267	393	deposed
Germanos IV	1842—1845	695	deposed
Germanos IV[2]	1852, 53	699	

Gregorios I (Theologos)	379—381	128	resigned
Gregorios II (Cyprius)	1283—1289	398	resigned
Gregorios III	1443—1450	466	deposed
Gregorios IV	1623	552	deposed
Gregorios V	1797, 98	675	deposed
Gregorios V²	1806—1808	680	deposed
Gregorios V³	1818—1821	684	hanged
Gregorios VI	1835—1840	692	deposed
Gregorios VI²	1867—1871	703	resigned
Hieremias I	1520—1522	500	deposed
Hieremias I²	1523—1527	502	deposed
Hieremias I³	1537—1545	505	
Hieremias II	1572—1579	518	deposed
Hieremias II²	1580—1584	524	deposed
Hieremias II³	1586—1595	531	
Hieremias III	1716—1726	622	deposed
Hieremias III²	1733	631	deposed
Hieremias IV	1809—1813	682	resigned
Ignatios	846—857	278	deposed
Ignatios²	867—878	287	
Isaac	1630	555	deposed
Isidoros I	1347—1350	422	resigned
Isidoros II	1456—1463	479	
Iacobos¹	1679—1683	603	deposed
Iacobos²	1685, 86	605	deposed
Iacobos³	1687, 88	606	resigned
Ioakim I	1498—1502	493	deposed
Ioakim I²	1504, 05	497	
Ioakim II	1860—1863	701	resigned
Ioakim II²	1873—1878	706	
Ioakim III	1878—1884	706	resigned
Ioannes I (Chrysostom)	398—404	141	deposed
Ioannes II	518—520	219	
Ioannes III	566—597	230	
Ioannes IV	582—595	232	
Ioannes V	668—674	247	
Ioannes VI	711—715	254	
Ioannes VII	832—842	274	deposed
Ioannes VIII	1064—1075	328	
Ioannes IX	1111—1134	348	
Ioannes X	1199—1206	377	resigned
Ioannes XI	1275—1282	394	deposed
Ioannes XII	1294—1303	404	resigned
Ioannes XIII	1315	415	resigned

Ioannes XIV	1334—1347	420	deposed
Ioannikios I	1522, 23	502	deposed
Ioannikios II	1646—1648	574	deposed
Ioannikios II[2]	1651, 52	575	resigned
Ioannikios II[3]	1653, 54	582	deposed
Ioannikios II[4]	1655, 56	584	deposed
Ioannikios III	1761—1763	654	deposed
Ioasaph I	1464—1466	481	deposed
Ioasaph II	1555—1565	510	deposed
Ioseph I	1268—1275	393	deposed
Ioseph II	1416—1439	464	
Laurentios	154—166	93	
Leon	1134—1143	350	
Leontios	1190, 91	374	deposed
Lucas	1156—1169	360	
Macarios	1376—1379	439	deposed
Macarios[2]	1390, 91	448	deposed
Macedonios I	342—348	118	
Macedonios I[2]	350—360	121	
Macedonios II	496—511	209	deposed
Manuel I	1215—1222	383	
Manuel II	1244—1255	388	
Marcos I	198—211	95	
Marcos II	1466, 67	481	deposed
Malthaios I	1397—1410	457	
Malthaios II	1595	536	resigned
Malthaios II[2]	1599—1602	541	resigned
Maximianos	431—434	179	
Maximos I	381	131	deposed
Maximos II	1215	382	
Maximos III	1476—1482	485	
Maximos IV	1491—1497	491	deposed
Meletios I	1597—1599	540	locum tenens
Meletios II	1768, 69	661	deposed
Meletios III	1845	696	
Menas	536—552	224	
Methodios I	842—846	277	
Methodios II	1240	387	
Methodios III	1668—1671	592	resigned
Metrophanes I	315—325	104	
Metrophanes II	1440—1443	465	deposed
Metrophanes III	1565—1572	515	deposed
Metrophanes III[2]	1579, 80	523	
Michael I	1043—1058	322	
Michael II	1143—1146	351	resigned
Michael III	1169—1177	365	
Michael IV	1206—1212	379	

Nectarios	381—397	133	
Neilos	1380—1388	440	
Neophytos I	1153	358	deposed
Neophytos II	1602, 03	542	deposed
Neophytos II²	1607—1612	545	deposed
Neophytos III	1636, 37	561	resigned
Neophytos IV	1688, 89	608	deposed
Neophytos V	1707	617	deposed
Neophytos VI	1734—1740	634	deposed
Neophytos VI²	1743, 44	638	deposed
Neophytos VII	1789—1794	671	deposed
Neophytos VII²	1798—1801	677	deposed
Nephon I	1311—1314	411	resigned
Nephon II	1486—1489	488	deposed
Nephon II²	1497, 98	492	deposed
Nephon II³	1502	495	resigned
Nestorios	428—431	174	deposed
Nicephoros I	806—815	267	deposed
Nicephoros II	1260, 61	391	
Nicetas I	766—780	263	
Nicetas II	1187—1190	373	deposed
Nicolaos I	895—906	295	deposed
Nicolaos I²	911—925	298	
Nicolaos II	984—995	313	
Nicolaos III	1084—1111	338	
Nicolaos IV	1147—1151	354	resigned
Olympianos	187—198	95	
Onesimos	54—68	89	
Pachomios I	1503, 04	496	deposed
Pachomios I²	1505—1514	498	poisoned
Pachomios II	1584, 85	526	
Paisios I	1652, 53	581	resigned
Paisios I²	1654, 55	583	resigned
Paisios II	1726—1733	628	deposed
Paisios II²	1740—1743	635	deposed
Paisios II³	1744—1748	639	resigned
Paisios II⁴	1751, 54	644	deposed
Parthenios I	1639—1644	569	
Parthenios II	1644, 45	572	deposed
Parthenios II²	1648—1651	576	poisoned
Parthenios III	1656, 57	585	
Parthenios IV	1657—1662	587	resigned
Parthenios IV²	1665—1667	591	
Parthenios IV³	1671	594	deposed
Parthenios IV⁴	1675, 76	598	deposed
Parthenios IV⁵	1684, 85	604	deposed
Paulos I	340, 41	111	deposed

Paulos I[2]	342—344	117	deposed
Paulos I[3]	348—350	119	strangled
Paulos II	641—652	243	
Paulos III	686—693	252	
Paulos IV	780—784	265	resigned
Pertinax	169—187	94	
Petros	652—664	245	
Philadelphos	211—214	96	
Philotheos	1354, 55	428	resigned
Philotheos[2]	1364—1376	431	
Photios	857—867	282	deposed
Photios[2]	878—886	290	deposed
Phravitas	489, 90	204	
Plutarchos	89—105	90	
Polycarpos I	71—89	90	
Polycarpos II	141—144	92	
Polyeuctos	956—970	307	
Probos	303—315	100	
Proclos	434—447	181	
Procopios	1785—1789	669	deposed
Pyrrhos	638—641	242	deposed
Pyrrhos[2]	651, 52	245	
Raphael I	1475, 76	484	deposed
Raphael II	1603—1607	543	deposed
Ruphinos	283, 84	98	
Samuel	1763—1768	657	deposed
Samuel[2]	1773, 74	663	deposed
Sedekion	105—114	91	
Seraphim I	1733, 34	632	deposed
Seraphim II	1757—1761	649	deposed
Sergios I	610—638	238	
Sergios II	999—1019	315	
Sisinios I	425—427	172	
Sisinios II	995—998	313	
Sophronios I	1463, 64	480	deposed
Sophronios II	1774—1780	664	
Sophronios III	1863—1866	702	deposed
Stachys	38—54	89	Rom. xvi. 9
Stephanos I	886—893	293	
Stephanos II	925—928	300	
Symeon	1472—1475	483	resigned
Symeon[2]	1482—1486	487	deposed
Tarasios	784—806	265	
Theodoros I	676—678	249	deposed
Theodoros I[2]	683—686	251	
Theodoros II	1213—1215	381	
Theodosios I	1178—1183	369	deposed

Theodosios II	1769—1773	661	deposed
Theodotos I	815—821	272	
Theodotos II	1151—1153	357	
Theoleptos I	1514—1520	499	
Theoleptos II	1585, 86	528	deposed
Theophanes I	1596, 97	538	
Theophanes II	1657	587	deposed
Theophylactos	933—956	303	
Thomas I	607—610	237	
Thomas II	665—668	246	
Timotheos I	511—548	215	
Timotheos II	1612—1621	549	poisoned
Titos	242—272	97	
Tryphon	928—931	300	deposed

The Patriarchs who (in the *Synaxaristes*, G. Ch. Raphtane, Zante, 1868) are numbered with the Saints—οἱ ἐν τοῖς Ἁγίοις—are

Alexander	August 30	Ioseph I	October 30
Anastasios	February 10	Leon	November 12
Anatolios	July 3	Macedonios II	April 25
Antonios III	February 12	Maximianos	April 24
Arsakios	October 11	Maximos I	November 17
Athanasios	October 28	Menas	August 25
Atticos	January 8	Methodios I	June 14
Callinicos	August 23	Metrophanes I	June 4
Callistos	June 20	Nectarios	October 11
Castinos	January 25	Nephon II	August 11
Constantinos	July 29	Nicephoros I	June 2
Cosmas	January 2	Nicolaos II	December 16
Cyriacos	October 27	Nicolaos III	May 16
Cyros	January 8	Paul I	November 6
Epiphanios	August 25	Paul II	August 30
Eutychios	April 6	Photios	February 6
Flavianos	February 16	Polyeuctos	February 5
Gennadios I	November 17	Proclos	November 20
Georgios I	August 18	Sisinios I	October 11
Germanos I	May 12	Stachys	October 31
Gregorios I	January 30	Stephanos I	May 18
Ignatios	October 23	Stephanos II	July 18
Ioannes I	November 13	Tarasios	February 25
Ioannes II	August 25 & 30	Theodoros I	December 27
Ioannes III	February 21	Thomas I	March 21
Ioannes V	August 18	Tryphon	April 19

Ἡ πρώτη στήλη σημειοῖ τὸ ὄνομα τοῦ Πατριάρχου· ἡ δευτέρα, τὸ ἔτος μ. Χ.· ἡ τρίτη τὴν σελίδα ἐν τῇ ἐκδόσει "M. I. Γεδεών, Πατριαρχικοὶ πίνακες, Κωνστ. 1890." Ἡ τετάρτη δηλοῖ πῶς ἔθετο τέρμα εἰς τὴν πατριαρχίαν του.

Ἀγαθάγγελος	1826—1830	688	παυθεὶς
Ἀκάκιος	471—489	198	
Ἀθανάσιος I	1289—1293	402	παραιτηθεὶς
Ἀθανάσιος I²	1303—1311	405	παραιτηθεὶς
Ἀθανάσιος II	1450	467	παραιτηθεὶς
Ἀθανάσιος III			
(Παντελλάριος)	1634	559	παυθεὶς
Ἀθανάσιος III²	1652	580	παραιτηθεὶς
Ἀθανάσιος IV	1679	602	παυθεὶς
Ἀθανάσιος V	1709—1711	619	παυθεὶς
Ἀθηνόδωρος	144—148	92	
Ἀλέξανδρος	325—340	108	
Ἀλέξιος	1025—1043	317	
Ἀλύπιος	166—169	94	
Ἀναστάσιος	730—754	259	
Ἀνατόλιος	449—458	188	
Ἀνδρέας, Ἀπ.			
Ἄνθιμος I	536	223	παυθεὶς
Ἄνθιμος II	1623	552	παραιτηθεὶς
Ἄνθιμος III	1822—1824	686	παυθεὶς
Ἄνθιμος IV			
(Βαμβάκης)	1840, 1841	694	παυθεὶς
Ἄνθιμος IV²	1848—1852	698	παυθεὶς
Ἄνθιμος V	1841, 1842	694	
Ἄνθιμος VI			
(Ἰωαννίδης)	1845—1848	697	παυθεὶς
Ἄνθιμος VI²	1853—1855	699	παυθεὶς
Ἄνθιμος VI³	1871—1873	705	παραιτηθεὶς
Ἀντώνιος I			
(Κασυματᾶς)	821—832	273	
Ἀντώνιος II			
(Καυλίας)	893—895	294	
Ἀντώνιος III			
(Στουδίτης)	974—980	310	παραιτηθεὶς
Ἀντώνιος IV			
(Μακάριος)	1389, 1390	448	παυθεὶς
Ἀντώνιος IV²	1391—1397	449	

Ἀρσάκιος	404, 405	161	
Ἀρσένιος	1255—1260	389	παραιτηθεὶς
Ἀρσένιος²	1261—1267	392	παυθεὶς
Ἄττικος	406—425	164	
Βασίλειος I			
(Σκαμανδρηνὸς)	970—974	309	παυθεὶς
Βασίλειος II			
(Καματηρὸς)	1183—1187	371	παυθεὶς
Γαβριὴλ I	1596	537	
Γαβριὴλ II	1657	586	παυθεὶς
Γαβριὴλ III	1702—1707	614	
Γαβριὴλ IV	1780—1785	666	
Γεννάδιος I	458—471	194	
Γεννάδιος II	1454—1456	471	παραιτηθεὶς
Γεράσιμος I	1320, 1321	417	
Γεράσιμος II	1673—1675	597	παυθεὶς
Γεράσιμος III	1794—1797	673	
Γερμανὸς I	715—730	255	παραιτηθεὶς
Γερμανὸς II	1222—1240	383	
Γερμανὸς III	1267	393	παυθεὶς
Γερμανὸς IV	1842—1845	695	παυθεὶς
Γερμανὸς IV²	1852, 1853	699	
Γεώργιος I			
(Σχολάριος)	678—683	250	παυθεὶς
Γεώργιος II			
(Ξιφιλῖνος)	1192—1199	376	
Γρηγόριος I			
(Θεολόγος)	379—381	128	παραιτηθεὶς
Γρηγόριος II			
(Κύπριος)	1283—1289	398	παραιτηθεὶς
Γρηγόριος III			
(Μάμμας)	1443—1450	466	παυθεὶς
Γρηγόριος IV			
(Στραβοαμασείας)	1623	552	παυθεὶς
Γρηγόριος V	1797, 1798	675	παυθεὶς
Γρηγόριος V²	1806—1808	680	παυθεὶς
Γρηγόριος V³	1818—1821	684	ἀπαγχονισθεὶς
Γρηγόριος VI	1835—1840	692	παυθεὶς
Γρηγόριος VI²	1867—1871	703	παραιτηθεὶς
Δημόφιλος	369—379	126	παυθεὶς
Διογένης	114—129	91	
Διονύσιος	1467—1472	482	παυθεὶς
Διονύσιος I²	1489—1491	490	παυθεὶς
Διονύσιος II	1537	504	παυθεὶς
Διονύσιος II²	1543—1555	507	
Διονύσιος III			
(Βάρδαλις)	1662—1665	588	παυθεὶς

Διονύσιος IV (Μουσελίμης)	1671—1673	595	παυθείς
Διονύσιος IV²	1676—1679	599	παυθείς
Διονύσιος IV³	1683, 84	604	παυθείς
Διονύσιος IV⁴	1686, 87	605	παυθείς
Διονύσιος IV⁵	1693	610	παυθείς
Δομέτιος	272—303	98	
Δοσίθεος	1191, 92	375	παυθείς
Ἐλευθέριος	129—136	91	
Ἐπιφάνιος	520—536	220	
Εὐάγριος	369, 70	127	παυθείς
Εὐδόξιος	360—369	122	
Εὐγένιος I	237—242	97	
Εὐγένιος II	1821, 22	686	
Εὐζώιος	148—154	93	
Εὐθύμιος I	906—911	296	παυθείς
Εὐθύμιος II	1410—1416	463	
Εὐσέβιος	341, 42	114	
Εὐστάθιος	1019—1025	317	
Εὐστράτιος	1081—1084	335	παυθείς
Εὐτύχιος	552—565	227	παυθείς
Εὐτύχιος²	577—582	231	
Εὐφήμιος	490—496	206	παυθείς
Ἡσαΐας	1323—1334	417	
Θεόδωρος I	676—678	249	παυθείς
Θεόδωρος I²	683—686	251	
Θεόδωρος II (Κωπᾶς)	1213—1215	381	
Θεοδόσιος I	1178—1183	369	παυθείς
Θεοδόσιος II (Μαριδάκης)	1769—1773	661	παυθείς
Θεόδοτος I	815—821	272	
Θεόδοτος II	1151—1153	357	
Θεόληπτος I	1514—1520	499	
Θεόληπτος II	1585, 86	528	παυθείς
Θεοφάνης I (Καρύκης)	1596, 97	538	
Θεοφάνης II	1657	587	παυθείς
Θεοφύλακτος	933—956	303	
Θωμᾶς I	607—610	237	
Θωμᾶς II	665—668	246	
Ἰάκωβος¹	1679—1683	603	παυθείς
Ἰάκωβος²	1685, 86	605	παυθείς
Ἰάκωβος³	1687, 88	606	παραιτηθείς
Ἰγνάτιος	846—857	278	παυθείς
Ἰγνάτιος²	867—878	287	
Ἱερεμίας I	1520—1522	500	παυθείς

Ἰερεμίας Ι²	1523—1527	502	παυθεὶς
Ἰερεμίας Ι³	1537—1545	505	
Ἰερεμίας ΙΙ (Τρανὸς)	1572—1579	518	παυθεὶς
Ἰερεμίας ΙΙ²	1580—1584	524	παυθεὶς
Ἰερεμίας ΙΙ³	1586—1595	531	
Ἰερεμίας ΙΙΙ	1716—1726	622	παυθεὶς
Ἰερεμίας ΙΙΙ²	1733	631	παυθεὶς
Ἰερεμίας ΙV	1809—1813	682	παραιτηθεὶς
Ἰσαὰκ	1630	555	παυθεὶς
Ἰσίδωρος Ι	1347—1350	422	παραιτηθεὶς
Ἰσίδωρος ΙΙ	1456—1463	479	
Ἰωακεὶμ Ι	1498—1502	493	παυθεὶς
Ἰωακεὶμ Ι²	1504, 1505	497	
Ἰωακεὶμ ΙΙ	1860—1863	701	παραιτηθεὶς
Ἰωακεὶμ ΙΙ²	1873—1878	706	
Ἰωακεὶμ ΙΙΙ	1878—1884	706	παραιτηθεὶς
Ἰωάννης Ι (Χρυσόστομος)	398—404	141	παυθεὶς
Ἰωάννης ΙΙ (Καππαδόκης)	518—520	219	
Ἰωάννης ΙΙΙ	566—577	230	
Ἰωάννης ΙV (Νηστευτὴς)	582—595	232	
Ἰωάννης V	668—674	247	
Ἰωάννης VΙ	711—715	254	
Ἰωάννης VΙΙ (Παγκρατίον)	832—842	274	παυθεὶς
Ἰωάννης VΙΙΙ (Ξιφιλῖνος)	1064—1075	328	
Ἰωάννης ΙΧ (Ἀγαπητὸς)	1111—1134	348	
Ἰωάννης Χ (Καματηρὸς)	1199—1206	397	παραιτηθεὶς
Ἰωάννης ΧΙ (Βέκκος)	1275—1282	394	παυθεὶς
Ἰωάννης ΧΙΙ (Κοσμᾶς)	1294—1303	404	παραιτηθεὶς
Ἰωάννης ΧΙΙΙ (Γλυκὺς)	1315	415	παραιτηθεὶς
Ἰωάννης ΧΙV (Καλέκας)	1334—1347	420	παυθεὶς
Ἰωαννίκιος Ι	1522, 23	502	παυθεὶς
Ἰωαννίκιος ΙΙ (Λίνδιος)	1646—1648	574	παυθεὶς
Ἰωαννίκιος ΙΙ²	1651, 52	575	παραιτηθεὶς
Ἰωαννίκιος ΙΙ³	1653, 54	582	παυθεὶς

Ἰωαννίκιος II[4]	1655, 56	584	παυθεὶς
Ἰωαννίκιος III (Καρατζᾶς)	1761—1763	654	παυθεὶς
Ἰωάσαφ I (Κόκκας)	1464—1466	481	παυθεὶς
Ἰωάσαφ II	1555—1565	510	παυθεὶς
Ἰωσὴφ I	1268—1275	393	παυθεὶς
Ἰωσὴφ I[2]	1283	397	
Ἰωσὴφ II	1416—1439	464	
Καλλίνικος I	693—705	253	τυφλωθεὶς
Καλλίνικος II (Ἀκαρνὰν)	1688	607	παυθεὶς
Καλλίνικος II[2]	1689—1693	609	παυθεὶς
Καλλίνικος II[3]	1694—1702	611	
Καλλίνικος III	1726	627	
Καλλίνικος IV	1757	648	παυθεὶς
Καλλίνικος V	1801—1806	679	παυθεὶς
Καλλίνικος V[2]	1808—1809	681	
Κάλλιστος I	1350—1354	426	παυθεὶς
Κάλλιστος I[2]	1355—1363	429	
Κάλλιστος II (Ξανθόπουλος)	1397	456	
Καστῖνος	230—237	97	
Κλήμης	1667	592	παυθεὶς
Κοσμᾶς I (Ἱεροσολυμίτης)	1075—1081	333	παραιτηθεὶς
Κοσμᾶς II	1146, 47	353	παυθεὶς
Κοσμᾶς III	1714—1716	621	παραιτηθεὶς
Κυπριανὸς I	1708, 09	617	παραιτηθεὶς
Κυπριανὸς I[2]	1713, 14	621	παραιτηθεὶς
Κυριακὸς I	214—230	96	
Κυριακὸς II	595—606	236	
Κύριλλος I (Λούκαρις)	1612	547	παραιτηθεὶς
Κύριλλος I[2]	1621—1623	550	παυθεὶς
Κύριλλος I[3]	1623—1630	553	παυθεὶς
Κύριλλος I[4]	1630—1634	556	παυθεὶς
Κύριλλος I[5]	1634, 35	560	παυθεὶς
Κύριλλος I[6]	1637, 38	562	πνιγεὶς
Κύριλλος II (Κονταρῆς)	1632	558	παυθεὶς
Κύριλλος II[2]	1635, 36	560	παυθεὶς
Κύριλλος II[3]	1638, 39	567	παυθεὶς
Κύριλλος III (Σπανὸς)	1652	579	παυθεὶς
Κύριλλος IV	1711—1713	620	παυθεὶς
Κύριλλος V (Καράκαλος)	1748—1751	641	παυθεὶς

Κύριλλος V²	1752—1757	644	παυθείς
Κύριλλος VI			
(Σερμπετσόγλους)	1813--1818	683	φονευθείς
Κύριλλος VII	1855—1860	669	παυθείς
Κῦρος	705—711	254	παυθείς
Κωνσταντῖνος I	674—676	248	
Κωνσταντῖνος II	754—766	262	τυφλωθείς καὶ ἀποκεφα-
Κωνσταντῖνος III			λισθείς
(Λευχούδης)	1059—1063	327	
Κωνσταντῖνος IV			
(Χλιαρηνὸς)	1154—1156	359	
Κωνστάντιος I	1830—1834	689	παραιτηθείς
Κωνστάντιος II	1834, 35	692	παυθείς
Λαυρέντιος	154—166	93	
Λέων	1134—1143	350	
Λεόντιος	1190, 91	374	παυθείς
Λουκᾶς	1156—1169	360	
Μακάριος	1376—1379	439	παυθείς
Μακάριος²	1390, 91	448	παυθείς
Μακεδόνιος I	342—348	118	παυθείς
Μακεδόνιος I²	350—360	121	
Μακεδόνιος II	496—511	209	παυθείς
Μανουὴλ I			
(Σαραντηνὸς)	1215—1222	383	
Μανουὴλ II	1244—1255	388	
Μάρκος I	198—211	95	
Μάρκος II			
(Ξυλοκαράβης)	1466, 67	481	παυθείς
Ματθαῖος I	1397—1410	457	
Ματθαῖος II	1595	536	παραιτηθείς
Ματθαῖος II²	1599—1602	541	παραιτηθείς
Μαξιμιανὸς	431—434	179	
Μάξιμος I	381	131	παυθείς
Μάξιμος II	1215	382	
Μάξιμος III	1476—1482	485	
Μάξιμος IV	1491—1497	491	παυθείς
Μεθόδιος I	842—846	277	
Μεθόδιος II	1240	387	
Μεθόδιος III			
(Μορώνης)	1668—1671	592	παραιτηθείς
Μελέτιος I (Πηγᾶς)	1597—1599	540	τοποτηρητὴς
Μελέτιος II	1768, 69	661	παυθείς
Μελέτιος III			
(Πάγκαλος)	1845	696	
Μηνᾶς	536--552	224	
Μητροφάνης I	315—325	104	
Μητροφάνης II	1440—1443	465	παυθείς

Μητροφάνης III	1565—1572	515	παυθείς
Μητροφάνης III²	1579, 80	523	
Μιχαὴλ I	1043—1058	322	
Μιχαὴλ II (Κουρκούας)	1143—1146	351	
Μιχαὴλ III (τοῦ Ἀγχιάλου)	1169—1177	365	
Μιχαὴλ IV (Αὐτωρειανὸς)	1206—1212	379	
Νεκτάριος	381—397	133	
Νεῖλος	1380—1388	440	
Νεόφυτος I	1153	358	παυθείς
Νεόφυτος II	1602, 03	542	παυθείς
Νεόφυτος II²	1607—1612	545	παυθείς
Νεόφυτος III	1636, 37	561	παραιτηθείς
Νεύφυτος IV	1688, 89	608	παυθείς
Νεόφυτος V	1707	617	παυθείς
Νεόφυτος VI	1734—1740	634	παυθείς
Νεόφυτος VI²	1743, 44	638	παυθείς
Νεόφυτος VII	1789—94	671	παυθείς
Νεόφυτος VII²	1798—1801	677	παυθείς
Νεστόριος	428—431	174	παυθείς
Νήφων I	1311—1314	411	παραιτηθείς
Νήφων II	1486—1489	488	παυθείς
Νήφων II²	1497, 98	492	παυθείς
Νήφων II³	1502	495	παραιτηθείς
Νικήτας I	766—780	263	
Νικήτας II (Μουντάνης)	1187—1190	373	παυθείς
Νικηφόρος I	806—815	267	παυθείς
Νικηφόρος II	1260, 61	391	
Νικόλαος I (Μυστικὸς)	895—906	295	παυθείς
Νικόλαος I²	911—925	298	
Νικόλαος II (Χρυσοβέργιος)	984—995	313	
Νικόλαος III (Γραμματικὸς)	1084—1111	338	
Νικόλαος IV (Μουζάλων)	1147—1151	354	παραιτηθείς
Ὀλυμπιανὸς	187—198	95	
Ὀνήσιμος	54—68	89	
Παΐσιος I	1652, 53	581	παραιτηθείς
Παΐσιος I²	1654, 55	583	παραιτηθείς
Παΐσιος II (Κιομουρτζόγλους)	1726—1733	628	παυθείς
Παΐσιος II²	1740—1743	635	

Παίσιος II³	1744—1748	639	παραιτηθεὶς
Παίσιος II⁴	1751, 52	644	παυθεὶς
Παρθένιος I			
(Γέρων)	1639—1644	569	
Παρθένιος II			
('Οξὺς)	1644, 45	572	παυθεὶς
Παρθένιος II²	1648—1651	576	δηλητηριασθεὶς
Παρθένιος III	1656, 57	585	
Παρθένιος IV			
(Μογιλάλος)	1657—1662	587	παραιτηθεὶς
Παρθένιος IV²	1665—1667	591	παυθεὶς
Παρθένιος IV³	1671	594	παυθεὶς
Παρθένιος IV⁴	1675, 76	598	παυθεὶς
Παρθένιος IV⁵	1684, 85	604	παυθεὶς
Παῦλος I	340, 41	111	παυθεὶς
Παῦλος I²	342—344	117	παυθεὶς
Παῦλος I³	348—350	119	ἀποπνιγεὶς
Παῦλος II	641—652	243	
Παῦλος III	686—693	252	
Παῦλος IV	780—784	265	παραιτηθεὶς
Παχώμιος I	1503, 04	496	
Παχώμιος I²	1505—1514	498	δηλητηριασθεὶς
Παχώμιος II			
(Πατέστος)	1584, 85	526	παυθεὶς
Περτίναξ	169—187	94	
Πέτρος	652—664	245	
Πλούταρχος	89—105	90	
Πολύευκτος	956—970	307	
Πολύκαρπος I	71—89	90	
Πολύκαρπος II	141—144	92	
Πρόβος	303—315	100	
Πρόκλος	434—447	181	
Προκόπιος	1785—1789	669	παυθεὶς
Πύῤῥος	638—641	241	παυθεὶς
Πύῤῥος²	651, 52	245	
'Ραφαὴλ I (Σέρβος)	1475, 76	484	παυθεὶς
'Ραφαὴλ II	1603—1607	543	παυθεὶς
'Ρουφῖνος	283, 84	98	
Σαμουὴλ¹	1763—1768	657	παυθεὶς
Σαμουὴλ²	1773, 74	663	παυθεὶς
Σεδεκίων	105—114	91	
Σεραφεὶμ I	1733, 34	632	παυθεὶς
Σεραφεὶμ II	1757—1761	649	παυθεὶς
Σέργιος I	610—638	238	
Σέργιος II	999—1019	315	
Σισίνιος I	425—427	172	
Σισίνιος II	995—998	313	

Στάχυς	38—54	89	῾Ρομ. xvi. 9
Στέφανος I	886—893	293	
Στέφανος II	925—928	300	
Συμεών	1472—1475	483	παραιτηθεὶς
Συμεών²	1482—1486	487	παυθεὶς
Σωφρόνιος I			
(Συρόπουλος)	1463, 64	480	παυθεὶς
Σωφρόνιος II	1774—1780	664	
Σωφρόνιος III	1863—1866	702	παυθεὶς
Ταράσιος	784—806	265	
Τιμόθεος I	511—548	215	
Τιμόθεος II	1612—1621	549	δηλητηριασθεὶς
Τῖτος	242—272	97	
Τρύφων	928—931	300	παυθεὶς
Φῆλιξ	136—141	91	
Φιλάδελφος	211—214	96	
Φιλόθεος	1354, 55	428	παραιτηθεὶς
Φιλόθεος²	1364—1376	431	
Φλαβιανὸς	447—449	185	φονευθεὶς
Φραυΐτας	489, 90	204	
Φώτιος	857—867	282	παυθεὶς
Φώτιος²	878—886	290	παυθεὶς
Χαρίτων	1177, 78	369	
Χρύσανθος	1824—1826	687	παυθεὶς

Οἱ ἐν τοῖς Ἁγίοις καταλεγόμενοι Πατριάρχαι (Συναξαριστής, Γ. Χ. Ῥαφτάνη, Ζάκυνθος, 1868) εἰσὶν οἱ ἀκόλουθοι.

Ἀθανάσιος	Ὀκτωβρίου 28	Κῦρος	Ἰανουαρίου 8
Ἀλέξανδρος	Αὐγούστου 30	Κωνσταντῖνος	Ἰουλίου 29
Ἀναστάσιος	Φεβρουαρίου 10	Λέων	Νοεμβρίου 12
Ἀνατόλιος	Ἰουλίου 3	Μακεδόνιος Β'	Ἀπριλίου 25
Ἀντώνιος Γ'	Φεβρουαρίου 12	Μαξιμιανὸς	Ἀπριλίου 4
Ἀρσάκιος	Ὀκτωβρίου 11	Μάξιμος Α'	Νοεμβρίου 17
Ἀττικὸς	Ἰανουαρίου 8	Μεθόδιος Α'	Ἰουνίου 14
Γεννάδιος Α'	Νοεμβρίου 17	Μηνᾶς	Αὐγούστου 25
Γεώργιος Α'	Αὐγούστου 18	Μητροφάνης Α'	Ἰουνίου 4
Γερμανὸς Α'	Μαΐου 12	Νεκτάριος	Ὀκτωβρίου 11
Γρηγόριος Α'	Ἰανουαρίου 30	Νήφων Β'	Αὐγούστου 11
Ἐπιφάνιος	Αὐγούστου 25	Νικηφόρος Α'	Ἰουνίου 2
Εὐτύχιος	Ἀπριλίου 6	Νικόλαος Β'	Δεκεμβρίου 16
Θεόδωρος Α'	Δεκεμβρίου 27	Νικόλαος Γ'	Μαΐου 16
Θωμᾶς Α'	Μαρτίου 21	Παῦλος Α'	Νοεμβρίου 6
Ἰγνάτιος	Ὀκτωβρίου 23	Παῦλος Β'	Αὐγούστου 30
Ἰωάννης Α'	Νοεμβρίου 13	Πολύευκτος	Φεβρουαρίου 5
Ἰωάννης Β'	Αὐγούστου 25 κ. 30	Πρόκλος	Νοεμβρίου 20
Ἰωάννης Γ'	Φεβρουαρίου 21	Σισίνιος Α'	Ὀκτωβρίου 11
Ἰωάννης Ε'	Αὐγούστου 18	Στάχυς	Ὀκτωβρίου 31
Ἰωσὴφ	Ὀκτωβρίου 30	Στέφανος Α'	Μαΐου 18
Καλλίνικος	Αὐγούστου 23	Στέφανος Β'	Ἰουλίου 18
Κάλλιστος	Ἰουνίου 20	Ταράσιος	Φεβρουαρίου 25
Καστῖνος	Ἰανουαρίου 25	Τρύφων	Ἀπριλίου 19
Κοσμᾶς	Ἰανουαρίου 2	Φλαβιανὸς	Φεβρουαρίου 16
Κυριακὸς	Ὀκτωβρίου 27	Φώτιος	Φεβρουαρίου 6

Printed in the United States
By Bookmasters